Academic Vocabulary Toolkit 1

Mastering High-Use Words for Academic Achievement

Dr. Kate Kinsella

Australia • Brazil • Japan • Korea • Mexico • Singapore • Spain • United Kingdom • United States

A Note from the Author

Dear Scholar,

Welcome to the *Academic Vocabulary Toolkit!*

I am so excited that you are going to have the opportunity to expand your vocabulary knowledge using this interactive program. To succeed in secondary school, college, and the workplace, you will need to have a powerful command of English vocabulary. The *Academic Vocabulary Toolkit* focuses on words that are used widely across different subject areas and careers in spoken and written communication. You will need to both understand and apply these practical words while participating in discussions, writing reports, and reading informational texts. I make these vocabulary "tools" a priority in my lessons with middle school and high school students so they will be prepared to achieve their educational and personal goals.

As you use this textbook in your classroom, you will probably notice that it is quite different from other textbooks that you have used before. Instead of quietly writing sentences in your notebook with your head down during class, your teacher will lead you through dynamic, engaging activities that require you to share your ideas with the class and with a partner. I want to make sure that you can use these critical words appropriately and that you enjoy the process of creating and collaborating with classmates.

When you use this interactive curricula in class, it's important that you listen carefully to your teacher. Your teacher will ask you to follow many directions, such as repeating a word or sentence or providing an answer for an activity. You will also have to listen carefully to your classmates and partners—together, you will brainstorm interesting, appropriate answers for different activities.

As the school year continues, you will find yourself using these advanced academic words more and more in class. You will participate regularly in class discussions and become more comfortable using academic language. In essence, you will find yourself becoming a scholar of the English language—and having fun at it, too!

You can do it!

My very best regards,

Dr. Kate

Kate Kinsella, Ed.D., is a teacher educator at San Francisco State University and a highly sought after speaker and consultant to school districts throughout the United States regarding development of academic language and literacy across the K–12 subject areas. Her 25-year teaching career focus has been equipping children from diverse backgrounds with the communication, reading, and writing skills to be career and college ready. Dr. Kinsella remains active in K–12 classrooms by providing in-class coaching and by teaching an academic literacy class for adolescent English Learners. Her extensive publishing career includes articles, chapters, English Learners' dictionaries, and reading intervention programs. A former Fulbright TESOL lecturer, Dr. Kinsella was co-editor of the *CATESOL Journal* from 2000–2005 and served on the editorial board of the TESOL Journal from 1999–2003. Dr. Kinsella lives in California with her family, including two young adopted children, Jane Dzung from Vietnam and John Carlos from Guatemala.

Table of Contents

Grammar Lessons

accurate
adjective

Academic Vocabulary Toolkit

Meaning	Example
exact, correct **Synonym:** precise **Antonym:** inaccurate	A _____ will give you an **accurate** measure of _____ .

Family

- **Noun:** accuracy
- **Adverb:** accurately

Word Partners

• _____ description	If you witness a crime, it's important to give the police an **accurate description** of what happened.
• _____ information	News journalists try to provide **accurate information** in their stories.
• _____ measurement	You can get an **accurate measurement** of your height and weight at the doctor's office.

Verbal Practice

Talk about It **Read** each sentence and **think** about how you would complete it.

Discuss your idea with your partner using the sentence frame.

Listen carefully to your partner's and classmates' ideas.

Write your favorite idea in the blank.

❶ My friend didn't give me **accurate** directions to the _____ , so I got lost.

❷ It's not as important to have **accurate** spelling and punctuation when you're writing a _____ as when you're writing an essay.

Writing Practice

Collaborate   **Work with your partner** to complete the sentence using **accurate** and appropriate content.

The movie _____ is not an _____ representation of life

because _____ .

Your Turn   **Work independently** to complete the sentence using **accurate** and appropriate content.

If I were to give an _____ description of my appearance, I would say that

I have _____ and _____ .

Be an   **Work independently** to write two sentences. In your first sentence, use **accurate** with a *plural noun*.
Academic   In your second sentence, use **accurate** with the word partner *accurate information*.
Author

❶ _____

_____

❷ _____

_____

> ## grammar tip
>
> **Adjectives do not have plural forms. Do not add an –s to adjectives when they describe plural nouns.**
>
> <u>accurate</u> facts
>
> <u>loud</u> dogs

Write an   **Complete** the paragraph using **accurate** and original content.
Academic
Paragraph

Hollywood movies about teens are usually not _____ representations
                                                            ❶

of life in middle or high school. These movies often feature stereotypical characters:

the _____ cheerleader, the nerdy outcast, the moody artist, and
          ❷

the _____ . While students like these certainly exist, it wouldn't
          ❸

be _____ to say that all teens match one of these descriptions. Another
          ❹

inaccurate feature of many teen movies is the way they depict students' responsibilities.

Teens in movies never seem to have homework or _____ ; they
                                                               ❺

only go to parties and _____ . Do you think these movies accurately
                              ❻

_____ your life at school?
          ❼

adequate

adjective

▶ **Say it:** ad • e • quate   **Write it:** _____

Meaning	Example
enough of something to fill a need **Synonym:** satisfactory **Antonym:** inadequate	I have an old _____ , but it is **adequate** for keeping me _____ during the winter.

Family

• *Adverb:* adequately

Word Partners

• _____ number of	Our school doesn't have an **adequate number of** lockers, so students have to share.
• _____ time	To finish the entire exam, you will need to budget **adequate time** for each section.
• lack _____	Many communities in the world **lack adequate** access to clean water.

Verbal Practice

Talk about It   **Read** each sentence and **think** about how you would complete it.

Discuss your idea with your partner using the sentence frame.

Listen carefully to your partner's and classmates' ideas.

Write your favorite idea in the blank.

❶ I hope that my grades are **adequate** for me to _____ this year.

❷ For an apology to be **adequate**, you have to _____ .

4

Writing Practice

Collaborate   **Work with your partner** to complete the sentence using **adequate** and appropriate content.

People need _____ amounts of _____ in order to be

happy and healthy.

Your Turn   **Work independently** to complete the sentence using **adequate** and appropriate content.

I don't need a new _____ because the one I have now is _____ .

Be an Academic Author   **Work independently** to write two sentences. In your first sentence, use **adequate** with the word partner *adequate number of*. In your second sentence, use **adequate** with the word partner *adequate time*.

❶ _____

_____

❷ _____

_____

> ### grammar tip
> **An adjective usually comes before the noun it describes.**
> an <u>adequate</u> excuse
> a <u>big</u> house
> a <u>green</u> jacket

Write an Academic Paragraph   **Complete** the paragraph using **adequate** and original content.

Most people know that a healthy diet should include an _____ ❶

number of fruits and vegetables, but do you know exactly how many of these foods you should

eat for _____ ❷ ? In 2011, the U.S. Department of Agriculture introduced

MyPlate, an icon that uses colored sections to demonstrate _____ ❸

portion sizes of fruits, vegetables, grains, proteins, and dairy. According to MyPlate, half

of every person's plate should have fruits and vegetables, while the other half should

_____ ❹ grains and proteins. A small serving of dairy, such as a cup

of milk or a slice of cheese, is considered _____ ❺ for one meal.

If you follow these dietary _____ ❻ and get plenty of exercise, you will

be _____ ❼ and fit for years to come.

5

advantage
noun

▶ **Say it:** ad • **van** • tage   ***Write it:*** _____

Meaning	Example	
a positive quality or benefit *Antonym:* disadvantage	Eagles have the **advantage** of _____ eyesight, which allows them to spot _____ from far away.	

Forms	Family
• *Singular:* advantage • *Plural:* advantages	• *Adjective:* advantageous

Word Partners	
• have an ____ over someone	Layla **has an advantage over** the other tennis players at school because she has been playing since she was 8 years old.
• take ____ of something	If you have the chance to travel abroad when you're young, you should **take advantage of** it.
• use something to (my/your/his/ her/our/their) ____	Mike studied Latin in middle school, and he **used it to his advantage** when studying Spanish in high school.

Verbal Practice

Talk about It **Read** each sentence and **think** about how you would complete it.

Discuss your idea with your partner using the sentence frame.

Listen carefully to your partner's and classmates' ideas.

Write your favorite idea in the blank.

❶ Being tall is an **advantage** in a sport like _____ .

❷ There are many **advantages** to having a large family, such as

_____ .

Writing Practice

Collaborate **Work with your partner** to complete the sentence using the correct form of **advantage** and appropriate content.

Fresh _____ juice has the _____ of tasting delicious

and being high in _____ .

Your Turn **Work independently** to complete the sentence using the correct form of **advantage** and appropriate content.

One _____ of living in a city is that _____ .

Be an Academic Author **Work independently** to write two sentences. In your first sentence, use **advantage** in the *singular form* and include a word partner. In your second sentence, use **advantage** in the *plural form*.

❶ _____

_____

❷ _____

_____

> ### grammar tip
>
> Count nouns name things that can be counted. Count nouns have two forms, singular and plural. To make most count nouns plural, add –*s*.
>
> Playing a sport has many advantage**s**.
>
> She answered the question**s**.

Write an Academic Paragraph **Complete** the paragraph using the correct form of **advantage** and original content.

There are many _____ to having a smart phone. For one,
❶

smart phones feature an Internet connection and access to applications that are

useful or _____ . For example, applications featuring
❷

_____ allow you to instantly access directions to any location.
❸

You can also look up local restaurants or _____ to visit. However,
❹

there are also some disadvantages to having a smart phone. For one, smart phones

are _____ , as are the monthly bills. Smart phones can also
❺

_____ people and cause them to ignore their friends, families, and
❻

surroundings. Overall, smart phones have many _____—as long as
❼

you don't become obsessed with them.

7

analysis
noun

▶ **Say it:** a • **nal** • y • sis   **Write it:** _____

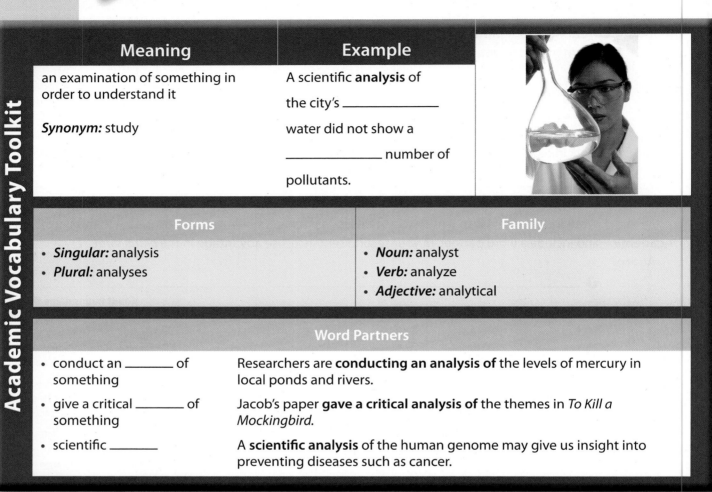

<table>
<tr><th colspan="2">Meaning</th><th colspan="2">Example</th></tr>
<tr><td colspan="2">an examination of something in order to understand it

Synonym: study</td><td colspan="2">A scientific **analysis** of the city's _____ water did not show a _____ number of pollutants.</td></tr>
<tr><th colspan="2">Forms</th><th colspan="2">Family</th></tr>
<tr><td colspan="2">• **Singular:** analysis
• **Plural:** analyses</td><td colspan="2">• **Noun:** analyst
• **Verb:** analyze
• **Adjective:** analytical</td></tr>
<tr><th colspan="4">Word Partners</th></tr>
<tr><td colspan="2">• conduct an _____ of something</td><td colspan="2">Researchers are **conducting an analysis of** the levels of mercury in local ponds and rivers.</td></tr>
<tr><td colspan="2">• give a critical _____ of something</td><td colspan="2">Jacob's paper **gave a critical analysis of** the themes in *To Kill a Mockingbird*.</td></tr>
<tr><td colspan="2">• scientific _____</td><td colspan="2">A **scientific analysis** of the human genome may give us insight into preventing diseases such as cancer.</td></tr>
</table>

Verbal Practice

Talk about It   **Read** each sentence and **think** about how you would complete it.

Discuss your idea with your partner using the sentence frame.

Listen carefully to your partner's and classmates' ideas.

Write your favorite idea in the blank.

❶ News journalists provide **analyses** of events around the world, such as

_____ .

❷ In English class, we had to give a critical **analysis** of _____ .

Writing Practice

Collaborate **Work with your partner** to complete the sentence using the correct form of **analysis** and appropriate content.

It would be interesting if our science class conducted an _____ of the

_____ near our school to determine whether or not it is polluted.

Your Turn **Work independently** to complete the sentence using the correct form of **analysis** and appropriate content.

When giving critical _____ of literary works such as _____ ,

you should consider the _____ in which they were written.

Be an Academic Author **Work independently** to write two sentences. In your first sentence, use **analysis** in the *plural form*. In your second sentence, use **analysis** in the *singular form* and include a word partner.

❶ _____

_____

❷ _____

_____

> **grammar tip**
>
> **Some nouns have irregular plural forms.**
>
> analysis—analyses
> child—children
> person—people

Write an Academic Paragraph **Complete** the paragraph using the correct form of **analysis** and original content.

DNA _____❶, or DNA fingerprinting, is a technique that scientists

have used since the late 1980s to identify people based on their DNA makeup. This process

begins by _____❷ a sample of DNA from a person, usually in the

form of saliva, blood, or hair. Scientists analyze the DNA in a laboratory and then use the

_____❸ to identify people. For instance, police investigators may want

to _____❹ that someone committed a crime by comparing the DNA of a

suspect to DNA that they _____❺ at a crime scene. Other times, people

want to know if they are related to _____❻ by comparing their DNA

to that person. DNA _____❼ is nearly 100 percent accurate, but it's not

foolproof—it is impossible to distinguish identical twins from one another using this method

because they share the same DNA.

9

analyze
verb

Academic Vocabulary Toolkit

Meaning	Example
to examine something in order to understand it *Synonym:* study	If you **analyze** a person's _____ , you can learn things about his or her _____ .

Forms		Family
Present: I/You/We/They analyze He/She/It analyzes		• *Nouns:* analysis, analyst • *Adjective:* analytical
Past: analyzed		

Word Partners

• _____ a book/painting/play/poem/story	It is often difficult to **analyze poems** because they contain complex language and symbolism.
• _____ data	Scientists **analyze data** in order to find patterns and draw conclusions.
• _____ a problem	The car mechanic will **analyze the problem** with the engine and then fix it.

Verbal Practice

Talk about It   **Read** each sentence and **think** about how you would complete it.

Discuss your idea with your partner using the sentence frame.

Listen carefully to your partner's and classmates' ideas.

Write your favorite idea in the blank.

❶ In science class this week, we are **analyzing**

_____ .

❷ I plan to **analyze** the difference between _____ and _____ for my English class.

Writing Practice

Collaborate **Work with your partner** to complete the sentence using the correct form of **analyze** and appropriate content.

Detectives _____ clues in order to solve _____ .

Your Turn **Work independently** to complete the sentence using the correct form of **analyze** and appropriate content.

In my _____ class, we recently _____ current events

in _____ .

Be an Academic Author **Work independently** to write two sentences. In your first sentence, use **analyze** in the *simple present tense*. In your second sentence, use **analyze** in the *present progressive tense* and include a word partner.

❶ _____

_____

❷ _____

_____

> **grammar tip**
>
> The present progressive tense is formed with *am/is/are* + a verb ending in *–ing*.
>
> The doctor <u>is analyzing</u> some blood samples.
>
> They <u>are running</u> laps.

Write an Academic Paragraph **Complete** the paragraph using the correct form of **analyze** and original content.

Everyone goes through difficult times in their _____ ❶ . When

this happens, many people visit professional therapists and counselors who help

them _____ ❷ their feelings and experiences and overcome

their problems. There are many reasons why people seek counseling; maybe their

_____ ❸ are getting divorced, or they've suffered a loss in their family.

Perhaps they have an eating disorder or are _____ ❹ depression.

A generation ago, it was not common for people to see a _____ ❺

or openly talk about their personal problems. However, today more and more people have

come to realize the benefits of _____ ❻ their problems with the

help of a professional. Going to therapy is not an easy experience, but it can significantly

_____ ❼ people's lives.

11

appropriate
adjective

<table>
<tr><th>Academic Vocabulary Toolkit</th><th colspan="2"></th></tr>
</table>

Meaning	Example
suitable or correct for a situation **Synonym:** acceptable **Antonym:** inappropriate	It's not **appropriate** to wear _____ to a formal _____ .

Family

- *Noun:* appropriateness
- *Adverb:* appropriately

Word Partners

• _____ behavior	Doing cartwheels may be **appropriate behavior** for the gym, but it is not allowed in the cafeteria.
• seems _____	Since many of the school buses regularly need repairs, it **seems appropriate** that the school district should buy replacements.
• take _____ measures	Our teacher **took appropriate measures** to make sure no students cheated on the quiz.

Verbal Practice

Talk about It **Read** each sentence and **think** about how you would complete it.

Discuss your idea with your partner using the sentence frame.

Listen carefully to your partner's and classmates' ideas.

Write your favorite idea in the blank.

❶ It's **appropriate** to wear _____ if you are going to the beach.

❷ You should always use **appropriate** language when speaking to your
_____ .

Writing Practice

Collaborate   **Work with your partner** to complete the sentence using **appropriate** and original content.

At our school, _____ clothes for students include _____

and _____ .

Your Turn   **Work independently** to complete the sentence using **appropriate** and original content.

When you eat at a restaurant, it is _____ to _____ .

Be an Academic Author   **Work independently** to write two sentences. In your first sentence, use **appropriate** with the word partner *appropriate behavior*. In your second sentence, use **appropriate** with a *plural noun*.

❶ _____

_____

❷ _____

_____

> **grammar tip**
>
> Adjectives do not have plural forms. Do not add an −*s* to adjectives when they describe plural nouns.
>
> <u>appropriate</u> clothes
>
> <u>loud</u> dogs

Write an Academic Paragraph   **Complete** the paragraph using **appropriate** and original content.

When traveling to another country, it's often difficult to know what kind of behavior is

_____ in different situations. In some countries, such as Mexico, it is
       ❶

considered insulting to refuse any food or drink your host _____ you.
                                                                              ❷

In Iran, on the other hand, it's _____ to refuse your host's offer two or
                                          ❸

three times before finally accepting. What clothing is considered _____
                                                                                   ❹

also _____ from country to country. In general, people in the United
            ❺

States dress informally. However, in other countries, such as France, people tend to dress much

more _____ and rarely wear shorts. Before you travel, you should make
             ❻

an effort to learn about local _____ so that you can better understand
                                   ❼

the culture of the country that you are visiting.

argue
verb

▶ **Say it:** **ar** • gue   **Write it:** _____

Meanings	Examples
1. to disagree or fight	**1.** The girl **argued** with her _____ because he forgot her _____ .
2. to give reasons for or against something	**2.** The _____ **argued** that her client was _____ because he had no motive to commit the crime.

Forms	Family
Present: I/You/We/They argue He/She/It argues **Past:** argued	• **Noun:** argument • **Adjective:** argumentative

Word Partners

• _____ for/against something	I would **argue against** raising the driving age to 18 because some students need to drive to school or to their jobs.
• _____ in favor of something	The students **argued in favor of** going on a field trip to the art museum.

Verbal Practice

Talk about It **Read** each sentence and **think** about how you would complete it.

Discuss your idea with your partner using the sentence frame.

Listen carefully to your partner's and classmates' ideas.

Write your favorite idea in the blank.

❶ Brothers and sisters often **argue** about _____ .

❷ I usually feel upset after I **argue** with my _____ .

❸ Some people think that rap music is _____ , but other people **argue** that it is an art form.

❹ If my friends and I could change anything about our school, we would **argue** in favor of _____ .

Writing Practice

Collaborate **Work with your partner** to complete the sentence using the correct form of **argue** and appropriate content.

Many vegetarians _____ against eating meat by saying that it is

_____ .

Your Turn **Work independently** to complete the sentence using the correct form of **argue** and appropriate content.

Some teachers _____ that students should take a lot of tests, but I think that

students should do more _____ to demonstrate what they know.

Be an **Work independently** to write two sentences using Meaning 2 of **argue**. In your first sentence, use
Academic **argue** in the *simple present tense* with a person's name. In your second sentence, use **argue** with the
Author modal verb *would* and include a word partner.

❶ _____

_____

❷ _____

_____

> ### grammar tip
>
> Modal verbs are helping verbs that give additional meaning to the main verb. *Would* can be used to express a preference.
>
> I **would argue** that football is a dangerous sport.
>
> He **would like** to meet her.

Write an **Complete** the paragraph using the correct form of **argue** and original content.
Academic
Paragraph Some parents _____ that teachers assign too much homework.
                              ❶

These parents _____ that completing large amounts of homework
                           ❷

every night causes students to feel _____ and keeps them from doing
                                        ❸

beneficial activities like _____ . However, other parents argue that
                            ❹

homework is important and helps students _____ what they learned
                                            ❺

in school. Certainly, some homework is _____ , but in general, most
                                         ❻

people would probably agree that too much homework is not _____
                                                           ❼

for students. Everyone can agree that it is important to help students achieve a healthy balance

between school and _____ .
                     ❽

argument
noun

▶ *Say it:* **ar** • gu • ment   *Write it:* _____

Meanings	Examples
1. a fight or disagreement	**1.** Carla had a _____ **argument** with her mother about what time she had to _____ .
2. a reason for or against something *Synonym:* claim	**2.** The congresswoman's persuasive **arguments** in favor of the law _____ Congress to pass it.

Forms	Family
• *Singular:* argument • *Plural:* arguments	• *Verb:* argue • *Adjective:* argumentative

Word Partners	
• persuasive ____	Avoiding a head injury is a **persuasive argument** for wearing a bicycle helmet.
• strong ____	One **strong argument** for drinking milk is that it strengthens your bones.
• support your ____	In a persuasive essay, you have to **support your argument** with facts or observations.

Verbal Practice

Talk about It   **Read** each sentence and **think** about how you would complete it.

Discuss your idea with your partner using the sentence frame.

Listen carefully to your partner's and classmates' ideas.

Write your favorite idea in the blank.

❶ I recently got into an **argument** with one of my friends because

_____ .

❷ During heated **arguments**, people sometimes _____

and regret it later.

❸ One strong **argument** against selling soda at school is that soda

_____ .

❹ The most persuasive **argument** for going to college is that

_____ .

Writing Practice

Collaborate **Work with your partner** to complete the sentence using the correct form of **argument** and appropriate content.

Two persuasive _____ against eating fast food are that fast food is

_____ and has high amounts of _____ .

Your Turn **Work independently** to complete the sentence using the correct form of **argument** and appropriate content.

A strong _____ for playing a sport is that it _____ .

Be an Academic Author **Work independently** to write two sentences using Meaning 2 of **argument**. In your first sentence, use **argument** in the *plural form*. In your second sentence, use **argument** in the *singular form* and include a word partner.

❶ _____

_____

❷ _____

_____

> ### grammar tip
>
> **Count nouns name things that can be counted. Count nouns have two forms, singular and plural. To make most count nouns plural, add –s.**
>
> Her arguments were convincing.
>
> He likes board games.

Write an Academic Paragraph **Complete** the paragraph using the correct form of **argument** and original content.

Many schools have banned students from having cell phones. One common

_____ that teachers make in support of this policy is that cell phones are
❶

disruptive. During class, students sometimes use their phones to _____
❷

instead of _____ . In addition, students can also use their phones to
❸

_____ on tests. However, one compelling _____
❹   ❺

that students make in favor of having cell phones is that they use their phones to keep in

touch with _____ before and after school. Students can also use their
❻

phones to look up _____ that they don't understand in class. These are
❼

all persuasive _____ that schools should consider before banning cell
❽

phones.

assume
verb

Academic Vocabulary Toolkit

Meaning	Example	
to think that something is probably true	If you see someone carrying a _____ , you might **assume** that he or she is in a _____ .	

Forms	Family
Present: I/You/We/They assume He/She/It assumes **Past:** assumed	• **Noun:** assumption • **Adjective:** assumed

Word Partners

• let's _____ that	**Let's assume that** we'll raise enough money for our trip and start planning it.
• reasonably _____	Based on the weather forecasts, we can **reasonably assume** that the hurricane will bring at least six inches of rain.

Verbal Practice

Talk about It   **Read** each sentence and **think** about how you would complete it.

Discuss your idea with your partner using the sentence frame.

Listen carefully to your partner's and classmates' ideas.

Write your favorite idea in the blank.

❶ If my mother didn't return my phone calls or text messages, I would **assume** that she was _____ .

❷ When I saw my friend running down the street, I **assumed** that he was _____ .

Writing Practice

Collaborate **Work with your partner** to complete the sentence using the correct form of **assume** and appropriate content.

Many adults tend to _____ that young people don't care about issues such

as _____ , even if they really do.

Your Turn **Work independently** to complete the sentence using the correct form of **assume** and appropriate content.

You should _____ that we will have to _____ in class

on Friday because it's usually required.

Be an Academic Author **Work independently** to write two sentences. In your first sentence, use **assume** in the *simple past tense*. In your second sentence, use **assume** with the modal verb *should*.

❶ _____

_____

❷ _____

_____

> **grammar tip**
>
> **Modal verbs are helping verbs that give additional meaning to the main verb. *Should* can be used to express advice.**
>
> You **should** assume that we'll have practice tomorrow.
>
> They **should stop** talking in class.

Write an Academic Paragraph **Complete** the paragraph using the correct form of **assume** and original content.

Many high school students _____ that getting good
                                              ❶

_____ and a high SAT score are the only things needed to get into
        ❷

college. While those accomplishments are important, most colleges are looking for

well-rounded students who _____ in a variety of extracurricular
                                        ❸

activities. They want to know: Are you a member of any school _____
                                                                           ❹

or sports teams? Are you a _____ individual who likes to
                                    ❺

draw or paint? Are you involved in any activities that benefit your community, such as

_____ ? You can't _____ a college knows who
        ❻   ❼

you are based on grades and test scores alone—you have to show them that you are special.

assumption

noun

▶ **Say it:** as • **sump** • tion   ***Write it:*** _____

<table>
<tr><td colspan="2">

Academic Vocabulary Toolkit

</td></tr>
<tr>
<th>Meaning</th>
<th>Example</th>
</tr>
<tr>
<td>

a belief about something that is not always true

Synonym: conclusion

</td>
<td>

We often make **assumptions** about people based on

_____ .

</td>
</tr>
</table>

Forms	Family
• ***Singular:*** assumption • ***Plural:*** assumptions	• ***Verb:*** assume • ***Adjective:*** assumed

Word Partners

• common _____	A **common assumption** about sharks is that they like to eat humans, but attacks are usually accidental.
• correct/false _____	Before they understood bacteria and viruses, doctors made many **false assumptions** about the causes of disease.
• make _____ s	Many people **make assumptions** before knowing all the facts.

Verbal Practice

Talk about It   **Read** each sentence and **think** about how you would complete it.

Discuss your idea with your partner using the sentence frame.

Listen carefully to your partner's and classmates' ideas.

Write your favorite idea in the blank.

❶ A negative **assumption** that people often make about dogs like pit bulls and Dobermans

is that they are _____ .

❷ One **assumption** that I made about this class before I took it was that

_____ .

Writing Practice

Collaborate **Work with your partner** to complete the sentence using the correct form of **assumption** and appropriate content.

It's not fair to make _____ about people you don't know based on how they

look or dress because _____ .

Your Turn **Work independently** to complete the sentence using the correct form of **assumption** and appropriate content.

One false _____ that people often make about me is that I am

_____ .

Be an Academic Author **Work independently** to write two sentences. In your first sentence, use **assumption** in the *singular form*. In your second sentence, use **assumption** in the *plural form*.

❶ _____

_____

❷ _____

_____

> **grammar tip**
>
> Count nouns name things that can be counted. Count nouns have two forms, singular and plural. To make most count nouns plural, add –*s*.
>
> His assumption**s** about me were wrong.
>
> She likes board games.

Write an Academic Paragraph **Complete** the paragraph using the correct form of **assumption** and original content.

Assumptions are judgments that help us _____ the world around us.
❶

People make _____ every day based on information they have learned
❷

in the past. For example, many drivers proceed through green lights without looking both ways

because they _____ that other drivers who have red lights will stop. This
❸

is a reasonable _____ because most drivers follow this rule. However,
❹

this assumption is also potentially _____ because there are times when
❺

drivers _____ red lights and cause accidents. It is important to think
❻

critically and determine whether your _____ about a situation are truly
❼

accurate.

aware
adjective

Write it: _____

<table>
<tr><td rowspan="4" style="writing-mode: vertical-rl;">**Academic Vocabulary Toolkit**</td></tr>
</table>

Academic Vocabulary Toolkit

Meaning	Example
knowing or noticing something **Synonym:** conscious of **Antonym:** unaware	The family was sound asleep in their _____ , so they weren't **aware** that a bear was outside _____ for food.

Family

• **Noun:** awareness

Word Partners

• acutely/vaguely _____	Tim was only **vaguely aware** that Leila liked him until she asked him to go on a date.
• fully _____	The librarian wants students to be **fully aware** of the services the library provides.
• well _____	After doing a research project on the subject, Jessica is **well aware** of the dangers of smoking.

Verbal Practice

Talk about It **Read** each sentence and **think** about how you would complete it.

Discuss your idea with your partner using the sentence frame.

Listen carefully to your partner's and classmates' ideas.

Write your favorite idea in the blank.

❶ If you're going to learn how to skateboard, it's important to be **aware** of

_____ .

❷ Since learning about it in social studies class, I am now fully **aware** of the fact that

_____ .

Writing Practice

Collaborate **Work with your partner** to complete the sentence using **aware** and appropriate content.

Groups like _____ try to make people more _____ of

problems such as _____ .

Your Turn **Work independently** to complete the sentence using **aware** and appropriate content.

Some people aren't _____ that I have a special ability to

_____ .

Be an Academic Author **Work independently** to write two sentences. In your first sentence, use **aware** with the word partner *well aware*. In your second sentence, use **aware** with the word partner *fully aware*.

❶ _____

_____

❷ _____

_____

> ### grammar tip
>
> Use *aware of* when the thing that is being noticed is a noun.
>
> I am well **aware of** the problem.
>
> We are fully **aware of** the danger.

Write an Academic Paragraph **Complete** the paragraph using **aware** and original content.

Bicycling is a _____ activity that can also be very dangerous
❶

if you're not fully _____ of how to do it safely. First, always
❷

wear a _____ that fits snugly on your head. Second, bike on
❸

the right side of the road or in a bike lane, and be _____ of
❹

parked cars. You should always _____ that drivers in moving
❺

and parked cars are unaware of your presence, so you need to pay close attention

to them. Third, at night, use a white light on the front of your bike and a red light on

the back of your bike, and wear light-colored or reflective _____ that
❻

helps drivers see you more easily. No matter how careful you are, accidents can still happen,

but you will be a lot safer if you _____ these recommendations.
❼

beneficial
adjective

▶ **Say it:** ben • e • **fi** • cial   **Write it:** _____

Meaning	Example
good or helpful	Drinking _____ is **beneficial** to your _____ .

Family

- **Noun:** benefit
- **Verb:** benefit
- **Adverb:** beneficially

Word Partners

- _____ effects   Eating fruits and vegetables has **beneficial effects** on your health.
- mutually _____   Humans and dogs have a **mutually beneficial** relationship.

Verbal Practice

Talk about It   **Read** each sentence and **think** about how you would complete it.

Discuss your idea with your partner using the sentence frame.

Listen carefully to your partner's and classmates' ideas.

Write your favorite idea in the blank.

❶ Having a pet is mutually **beneficial** for both the animal and the owner because

_____ .

❷ Before an important game, it's **beneficial** for athletes to

_____ .

24

Writing Practice

Collaborate **Work with your partner** to complete the sentence using **beneficial** and appropriate content.

If a student is having personal problems, it can be _____ for him or her to talk

to a _____ because _____ .

Your Turn **Work independently** to complete the sentence using **beneficial** and appropriate content.

One _____ effect of joining a club at school is that you might

_____ .

Be an Academic Author **Work independently** to write two sentences. In your first sentence, use **beneficial** with a *plural noun*. In your second sentence, use **beneficial** with a *singular noun*.

❶ _____

_____

❷ _____

_____

> ### grammar tip
> **Adjectives do not have plural forms. Do not add an –s to adjectives when they describe plural nouns.**
> beneficial effects
> loud dogs

Write an Academic Paragraph **Complete** the paragraph using **beneficial** and original content.

Many students feel that they _____ from having a
                                        ❶

study partner throughout the school year. Having a study partner can be mutually

_____ for a number of reasons. First, a study partner can help you
        ❷

catch up on _____ that you missed and remind you about upcoming
                        ❸

_____ . Second, your study partner may be able to help you
        ❹

_____ a variety of skills outside of the classroom, including conducting
        ❺

research or proofreading your papers. Finally, a study partner can _____
                                                                                    ❻

you to stay focused on your studies. You and your partner don't have to study the same subject;

sometimes it is _____ just to be in the same room with someone who is
                            ❼

also focusing on their studies. Do you think you would benefit from having a study partner?

benefit
noun

Academic Vocabulary Toolkit

Meaning	Example	
a positive result that you get from something	When you work out at a _____, you can quickly see the _____ **benefits**.	

Forms	Family
• *Singular:* benefit • *Plural:* benefits	• *Verb:* benefit • *Adjective:* beneficial • *Adverb:* beneficially

Word Partners

• health _____	Wearing sunscreen can provide many **health benefits** such as preventing sunburns and skin cancer.
• major _____	One **major benefit** of being a student is that you can get discounts at many restaurants and stores if you show your student ID card.
• reap the _____ s	If you study hard and complete all your homework, you will **reap the benefits** at school.

Verbal Practice

Talk about It   **Read** each sentence and **think** about how you would complete it.

Discuss your idea with your partner using the sentence frame.

Listen carefully to your partner's and classmates' ideas.

Write your favorite idea in the blank.

❶ _____ is a major **benefit** of having a part-time job or internship.

❷ One health **benefit** of eating fruits and vegetables is that they can help you _____ .

Writing Practice

Collaborate Work with your partner to complete the sentence using the correct form of **benefit** and appropriate content.

One _____ of texting rather than making a phone call is that

_____ .

Your Turn Work independently to complete the sentence using the correct form of **benefit** and appropriate content.

There are many _____ to starting a savings account, such as having money

for _____ .

Be an Academic Author Work independently to write two sentences. In your first sentence, use **benefit** in the *plural form* with the quantifier *many*. In your second sentence, use **benefit** in the *singular form*.

❶ _____

_____

❷ _____

_____

> ## grammar tip
>
> **Quantifiers are words that tell us how much or how many of something there is. They usually come before the noun they describe.**
>
> There are **many** benefits to participating in theater.
>
> I have **several** coins.

Write an Academic Paragraph Complete the paragraph using the correct form of **benefit** and original content.

There are a variety of ways in which students benefit from having computers at school.

One _____ is that they can watch video clips in class about
    ❶

topics that they are currently studying, such as _____ .
    ❷

Another _____ is that students can use computers to
    ❸

_____ and research papers. Just a few decades ago, students relied
    ❹

on the limited _____ at a library to research a topic. Now, they can
    ❺

go online and use search engines such as _____ to find information.
    ❻

Students can also use computers to check for errors in _____ as they
    ❼

write. There are numerous ways for students to use computers for educational purposes, and

as technology progresses, there will be even more _____ in the future.
    ❽

cause
noun

▶ **Say it:** cause   **Write it:** _____

Meanings	Examples
1. the reason why something happens	**1.** The **cause** of the car accident was that the _____ ran through a _____ .
2. a goal that people support and work toward	**2.** A clean _____ is important. I support this **cause** by picking up _____ .

Forms	Family
• *Singular:* cause • *Plural:* causes	• *Verb:* cause • *Adjective:* causal

Word Partners	
• _____ and effect	There is a **cause and effect** for every action that happens.
• determine the _____	My parents are trying to **determine the cause** of the flood in our basement.

Verbal Practice

Talk about It **Read** each sentence and **think** about how you would complete it.

Discuss your idea with your partner using the sentence frame.

Listen carefully to your partner's and classmates' ideas.

Write your favorite idea in the blank.

❶ Two **causes** of stress in my life are _____ and _____ .

❷ When my friend's MP3 player suddenly _____ , he didn't know the **cause**.

❸ _____ is a **cause** I support because I think that it affects everyone.

❹ Laura took up the **cause** of ending _____ by volunteering at a local food bank.

Writing Practice

Collaborate | **Work with your partner** to complete the sentences using the correct form of **cause** and appropriate content.

1. Before we can solve the problem of _____ , we must determine

   the _____ .

2. When our school announced it was removing _____ from the

   lunch menu, we took up the _____ of getting it back.

Your Turn | **Work independently** to complete the sentences using the correct form of **cause** and appropriate content.

1. We are studying the _____ and effects of war in _____ .

2. Improving _____ is a _____

   that many people in my community care about.

Be an Academic Author | **Work independently** to write two sentences. In your first sentence, use **cause** in the *plural form*. In your second sentence, use **cause** in the *singular form*.

MEANING 1 _____

_____

MEANING 2 _____

_____

> ## grammar tip
> **Count nouns name things that can be counted. Count nouns have two forms, singular and plural. To make most count nouns plural, add –*s*.**
>
> Crime has many cause**s**.
>
> She loves animal**s**.

Write an Academic Paragraph | **Complete** the paragraph using the correct form of **cause** and original content.

   Forensics is a _____ ❶ in which investigators use science to determine

the _____ ❷ of accidents, injuries, and deaths. Forensic investigators

are trained to _____ ❸ and analyze clues from the scene of an event.

One type of forensic expert is a crime scene investigator. These experts work with police

to figure out the _____ ❹ of crimes. Crime scene investigators are

important because they help police _____ ❺ crimes and identify

_____ ❻ who have committed crimes. Being a crime scene investigator is

just one _____ ❼ of career in forensics—there are dozens of others, all of

which require years of education and training.

cause
verb

Academic Vocabulary Toolkit

Meaning	Example	
to make something happen	Studying for _____ **causes** me to feel very _____ .	

Forms		Family
Present: I/You/We/They cause He/She/It causes **Past:** caused		• **Noun:** cause • **Adjective:** causal

Word Partners

- _____ damage — The tornado **caused damage** to most of the houses in my neighborhood.
- _____ harm — Some researchers suspect that cell phones are **causing harm** to our brains.
- _____ problems — If you **cause problems** in class, the teacher may give you detention or a referral.

Verbal Practice

Talk about It   **Read** each sentence and **think** about how you would complete it.

Discuss your idea with your partner using the sentence frame.

Listen carefully to your partner's and classmates' ideas.

Write your favorite idea in the blank.

❶ Many chemicals and pollutants in the world, such as _____,
are **causing** people to become sick.

❷ Sometimes _____ **causes** me to get distracted when I study.

Writing Practice

Collaborate   **Work with your partner** to complete the sentence using the correct form of **cause** and appropriate content.

_____ is _____

environmental problems in some parts of the world.

Your Turn   **Work independently** to complete the sentence using the correct form of **cause** and appropriate content.

_____ too much _____ can _____

harm to your body.

Be an Academic Author   **Work independently** to write two sentences. In your first sentence, use **cause** in the *present progressive tense*. In your second sentence, use **cause** in the *simple present tense* and include a word partner.

❶ _____

_____

❷ _____

_____

> ### grammar tip
>
> The present progressive tense is formed with *am/is/are* + a verb ending in *–ing*.
>
> This music <u>is causing</u> me to get distracted.
>
> They <u>are running</u> down the street.
>
> I <u>am acting</u> in a play.

Write an Academic Paragraph   **Complete** the paragraph using the correct form of **cause** and original content.

Taking tests _____❶_____ anxiety for many students. In fact, some

students _____❷_____ so overwhelmed during tests that it

_____❸_____ them to fail or perform poorly. These students may experience

_____❹_____ feelings of nausea or the sensation that they are going to faint.

Psychologists have determined that test-taking anxiety is a _____❺_____

of performance anxiety. This anxiety is accompanied by a sudden rush of adrenaline that

_____❻_____ students to feel debilitating physical sensations during tests. If

anxiety is affecting your performance on _____❼_____ , talk to your teachers or a

guidance counselor. They may be able to help you pinpoint the _____❽_____ of

your anxiety and help you overcome your problem.

31

challenge
noun

Say it: **chal** • lenge

Write it: _____

Meaning	Example	
a difficult task that requires a lot of effort	Sasha knew it would be a major **challenge** to win the _____ competition.	

Forms	Family
• *Singular:* challenge • *Plural:* challenges	• *Verb:* challenge • *Adjective:* challenging

Word Partners

• face a/the _____	Many families **face the challenge** of finding enough money to send their children to college every year.
• major _____	Climbing Mount Everest would be a **major challenge** for anyone.
• present a _____	Public speaking **presents a challenge** for many people.

Verbal Practice

Talk about It   **Read** each sentence and **think** about how you would complete it.

Discuss your idea with your partner using the sentence frame.

Listen carefully to your partner's and classmates' ideas.

Write your favorite idea in the blank.

❶ For many new immigrants, one of the biggest **challenges** they face is

_____ .

❷ One major **challenge** that children present to babysitters is refusing to

_____ .

Writing Practice

Collaborate   **Work with your partner** to complete the sentence using the correct form of **challenge** and appropriate content.

_____ is a subject that often presents a _____ to students

because _____ .

Your Turn   **Work independently** to complete the sentence using the correct form of **challenge** and appropriate content.

Two major _____ that I have had to overcome in my life are

_____ and _____ .

Be an Academic Author   **Work independently** to write two sentences. In your first sentence, use **challenge** in the *plural form*. In your second sentence, use **challenge** in the *singular form* and include a word partner.

❶ _____

_____

❷ _____

_____

> ### grammar tip
> Count nouns name things that can be counted. Count nouns have two forms, singular and plural. To make most count nouns plural, add –*s*.
>
> He has overcome many challenge**s** at school.
>
> She loves animal**s**.

Write an Academic Paragraph   **Complete** the paragraph using the correct form of **challenge** and original content.

Sometimes finding interesting reading material is a _____
❶

for students. However, there are a number of resources available that make it

_____ to find fun, engaging reading material. First, talk to the
❷

librarians at your _____ library about new materials that are available.
❸

Librarians can help you find a wide variety of resources—books, magazines, graphic novels,

online articles, and more—that focus on the _____ that you find
❹

interesting. Next, try typing "best-selling books for teens" in an online search engine to

_____ popular books that students your age are reading. Finally, talk
❺

to your _____ and ask them for reading recommendations. Reading is
❻

a fun, important _____ that will help you succeed in school and life.
❼

33

challenging
adjective

Academic Vocabulary Toolkit

Meaning	Example
difficult or requiring a lot of effort	Yoga may look _____ , but it's actually very **challenging**.

Family

- *Noun:* challenge
- *Verb:* challenge

Word Partners

• _____ task	If you are assigned a **challenging task** in class, you should ask your teacher or a classmate for help.
• find something _____	I **find dancing challenging** because I don't have any rhythm.
• most _____	The **most challenging** part of being a student is balancing your school and social lives.

Verbal Practice

Talk about It **Read** each sentence and **think** about how you would complete it.

Discuss your idea with your partner using the sentence frame.

Listen carefully to your partner's and classmates' ideas.

Write your favorite idea in the blank.

❶ _____ is the most **challenging** activity I've ever tried.

❷ Trying to juggle personal responsibilities, such as _____

and _____ , can be **challenging**.

Writing Practice

Collaborate **Work with your partner** to complete the sentence using **challenging** and appropriate content.

One of the most _____ issues facing young people today is

_____ because it _____ .

Your Turn **Work independently** to complete the sentence using **challenging** and appropriate content.

I recently completed a _____ project for school—I had to

_____ .

Be an Academic Author **Work independently** to write two sentences. In your first sentence, use **challenging** with a *plural noun*. In your second sentence, use **challenging** with the word partner *challenging task*.

❶ _____

_____

❷ _____

_____

> ## grammar tip
>
> **Adjectives do not have plural forms. Do not add an –s to adjectives when they describe plural nouns.**
>
> <u>challenging</u> activities
>
> <u>loud</u> dogs

Write an Academic Paragraph **Complete** the paragraph using **challenging** and original content.

   Challenging yourself is an _____ part of life because it can help you

grow as a person. There are many _____ tasks that students encounter

in their everyday lives that are actually quite rewarding. For example, a major school project

like a _____ might seem challenging at first, but after you

complete it, you'll have a great feeling of accomplishment. Some students even like

to _____ themselves by doing crossword puzzles, guessing the

_____ on game shows, and completing quizzes online. These types

of _____ activities train your brain to think in new ways and

may even help you perform better in school. So, the next time that a task seems too

_____ , try to see it as a challenge rather than a problem.

character
noun

Write it: _____

Academic Vocabulary Toolkit

Meanings	Examples
1. a person in a story, movie, or play	1. My favorite _____ has many interesting **characters**.
2. the features that make a person or thing unique	2. My aunt's _____ is painted bright _____ , which gives it a lot of **character**.

Forms	Family
• *Singular:* character • *Plural:* characters	• *Noun:* characteristic • *Verb:* characterize

Word Partners

- ____ trait — Good leaders share **character traits** such as fairness and respect for others.
- fictional ____ — The **fictional characters** in a story are what make it interesting.
- main ____ — Wilbur and Charlotte are the **main characters** in the novel *Charlotte's Web*.

Verbal Practice

Talk about It **Read** each sentence and **think** about how you would complete it.

Discuss your idea with your partner using the sentence frame.

Listen carefully to your partner's and classmates' ideas.

Write your favorite idea in the blank.

1. The main **character** in the last movie I saw was _____ .

2. When I was younger, my favorite cartoon **character** was _____ .

3. A firefighter needs to have the **character** trait of _____ .

4. I usually cover the outside of my notebooks with _____ , which gives them a lot of **character**.

Writing Practice

Collaborate **Work with your partner** to complete the sentences using the correct form of **character** and appropriate content.

❶ The most interesting _____ that I have read about or seen in a movie

recently is _____ from _____ .

❷ My bedroom has a lot of _____ because it has _____ .

Your Turn **Work independently** to complete the sentences using the correct form of **character** and appropriate content.

❶ The fictional _____ that I relate to the most is _____ .

❷ My _____ has an admirable _____ because

_____ .

Be an Academic Author **Work independently** to write two sentences. In your first sentence, use **character** in the *plural form*. In your second sentence, use **character** in the *singular form*.

MEANING ❶ _____

_____

MEANING ❷ _____

_____

grammar tip

Count nouns name things that can be counted. Count nouns have two forms, singular and plural. To make most count nouns plural, add –s.

I like the character**s** on this show.

He likes board games.

Write an Academic Paragraph **Complete** the paragraph using the correct form of **character** and original content.

Playing a _____ in a movie or TV show is an interesting and
❶

challenging job for actors. First, they have to _____ what the
❷

character is like. What kinds of _____ traits does their character have?
❸

Is the character always laughing and _____ , or is the character a
❹

_____ , someone who lies and steals? When actors play a part, they have
❺

to forget their own _____ and become someone who is completely
❻

different. Playing a _____ allows actors to explore various personality
❼

types and pretend to be someone they're not.

characteristic
noun

Say it: char • ac • ter • **is** • tic   **Write it:** _____

<table>
<tr><th colspan="2" style="text-align:center">Academic Vocabulary Toolkit</th></tr>
</table>

Meaning	Example
a quality or feature of a person or thing **Synonym:** trait	One **characteristic** of the ocean is that it is very _____ .

Forms	Family
• *Singular:* characteristic • *Plural:* characteristics	• *Verb:* characterize • *Adjective:* characteristic • *Adverb:* characteristically

Word Partners	
• common _____	A **common characteristic** of babies is that they cry frequently.
• key _____	Feathers are a **key characteristic** of birds.
• share a/the _____	All of the Murphy children **share the characteristics** of red hair and freckles.

Verbal Practice

Talk about It **Read** each sentence and **think** about how you would complete it.

Discuss your idea with your partner using the sentence frame.

Listen carefully to your partner's and classmates' ideas.

Write your favorite idea in the blank.

❶ My friends and I share a **characteristic:** we all like

_____ .

❷ One key **characteristic** that I like about my house is that it

_____ .

Writing Practice

Collaborate **Work with your partner** to complete the sentence using the correct form of **characteristic** and appropriate content.

_____ is the most important _____ of a good movie.

Your Turn **Work independently** to complete the sentence using the correct form of **characteristic** and appropriate content.

Two key _____ of my appearance are that I have _____

and that I often wear _____ .

Be an
Academic
Author

Work independently to write two sentences. In your first sentence, use **characteristic** in the *singular form*. In your second sentence, use **characteristic** in the *plural form* and include a word partner.

❶ _____

_____

❷ _____

_____

> ### grammar tip
>
> **Count nouns name things that can be counted. Count nouns have two forms, singular and plural. To make most count nouns plural, add –s.**
>
> Identical twins share physical characteristics.
>
> He likes board games.

Write an
Academic
Paragraph

Complete the paragraph using the correct form of **characteristic** and original content.

What are the most important characteristics of a good friend? Every friendship is different,

but there are a few common _____ that everyone should have in
                                          ❶

order to be a trusted friend. First, it is _____ to be an attentive listener.
                                                          ❷

Second, you need to spend enough _____ with your friends. Third, a key
                                                      ❸

_____ of a good friend is honesty. A good friend is someone who listens
          ❹

to their friends' _____ , gives honest _____ ,
                              ❺   ❻

and makes plenty of time to _____ with their friends. If your friends
                                              ❼

share these _____ , you have probably chosen good friends.
                      ❽

compare
verb

▶ **Say it:** com • **pare**   **Write it:** _____

Academic Vocabulary Toolkit

Meaning	Example	
to look at what is the same and what is different between two things	The students **compared** their _____ after the test.	

Forms	Family
Present: I/You/We/They compare He/She/It compares **Past:** compared	• **Noun:** comparison • **Adjective:** comparable • **Adverb:** comparatively

Word Partners

- _____ and contrast   Writing assignments often ask you to **compare and contrast** two things you have read about.

- _____ notes   Before a big test, I usually **compare notes** with my study partner.

- _____ results   The students **compared results** from their science experiments.

Verbal Practice

Talk about It   **Read** each sentence and **think** about how you would complete it.

Discuss your idea with your partner using the sentence frame.

Listen carefully to your partner's and classmates' ideas.

Write your favorite idea in the blank.

❶ It would be interesting to **compare** and contrast popular fashion styles in the United States with popular fashion styles in _____ .

❷ I **compared** the _____ habits of six-year-olds to those of teenagers.

Writing Practice

Collaborate | **Work with your partner** to complete the sentence using the correct form of **compare** and appropriate content.

It isn't healthy to _____ yourself to celebrities because sometimes they

_____ .

Your Turn | **Work independently** to complete the sentence using the correct form of **compare** and appropriate content.

People often _____ the singer _____ to the singer

_____ because they both _____ .

Be an Academic Author | **Work independently** to write two sentences. In your first sentence, use **compare** with the adverb of frequency *often*. In your second sentence, use **compare** in the *simple past tense* and include a word partner.

1 _____

_____

2 _____

_____

> ### grammar tip
> Adverbs of frequency are words that show how often something happens. They usually go before the main verb.
>
> People **often compare** twins.
>
> He **frequently arrives** late.

Write an Academic Paragraph | **Complete** the paragraph using the correct form of **compare** and original content.

Studies have shown that when people read magazines, they compare themselves

to the _____ **1** _____ in the photographs. This can be a very

_____ **2** _____ habit since magazine pictures are often heavily airbrushed.

Airbrushing is a process in which a _____ **3** _____ is digitally altered so that

the subject looks better. For example, _____ **4** _____ and skin flaws disappear,

and people can even be made to look thinner! When people _____ **5** _____

themselves to the models in airbrushed pictures, this can make them feel self-conscious about

their appearance. However, it is unrealistic to _____ **6** _____ a real person with

an airbrushed photograph. Instead, it's better to _____ **7** _____ your own body

image and not compare yourself to other people.

41

comparison
noun

Academic Vocabulary Toolkit

Meaning	Example
a study of the way that two things are the same and different	Florida is _____ most of the year. In **comparison**, New York is very _____ during the fall and winter.

Forms	Family
• **Singular:** comparison • **Plural:** comparisons	• **Verb:** compare • **Adjective:** comparable • **Adverb:** comparatively

Word Partners	
• draw a _____ between	It's easy to **draw comparisons between** identical twins.
• in _____	My bedroom is small **in comparison** to my parents' bedroom.
• make a _____ between	In our science class, our teacher **made a comparison between** white and red blood cells.

Verbal Practice

Talk about It   **Read** each sentence and **think** about how you would complete it.

Discuss your idea with your partner using the sentence frame.

Listen carefully to your partner's and classmates' ideas.

Write your favorite idea in the blank.

❶ One **comparison** you could draw between hip hop music and poetry is that both _____ .

❷ _____ is a talented celebrity; in **comparison**, _____ is not talented at all.

Writing Practice

Collaborate   **Work with your partner** to complete the sentence using the correct form of **comparison** and appropriate content.

The food that is served in our school cafeteria is _____ . In

_____ , the food that I eat at home is _____ .

Your Turn   **Work independently** to complete the sentence using the correct form of **comparison** and appropriate content.

People often make _____ between my _____

and me because we both _____ .

Be an Academic Author   **Work independently** to write two sentences. In your first sentence, use **comparison** in the *singular form* and include a word partner. In your second sentence, use **comparison** in the *plural form*.

❶ _____

_____

❷ _____

_____

> ## grammar tip
>
> **Count nouns name things that can be counted. Count nouns have two forms, singular and plural. To make most count nouns plural, add –s.**
>
> It's easy to make comparison**s** between rats and mice.
>
> He likes board game**s**.

Write an Academic Paragraph   **Complete** the paragraph using the correct form of **comparison** and original content.

Many people like to make _____ between family members.
❶

When babies are born, people enjoy _____ the baby to his or her
❷

_____ . You can make comparisons based on physical appearance, such
❸

as if a mother and daughter both have _____ , or you can base them
❹

on personality, such as if a father and son are both _____ by nature.
❺

Anyone with brothers or sisters will be used to hearing _____ ; people
❻

like to distinguish between siblings by saying which child is more outgoing or which child is more

_____ . It's fun to make comparisons about other people, but it's also
❼

important to remember that every person is a _____ individual.
❽

conclude
verb

Write it: _____

<table>
<tr><th colspan="2">Meanings</th><th>Examples</th></tr>
</table>

Academic Vocabulary Toolkit

Meanings	Examples
1. to finish *Synonym:* end	1. The concert **concluded** with a special _____ show that made the audience _____ .
2. to make a decision or form an opinion about something *Synonyms:* decide, determine	2. When Sarah saw that the dog was wagging its _____ , she **concluded** that it was _____ .

Forms		Family
Present: I/You/We/They conclude He/She/It concludes *Past:* concluded		• *Noun:* conclusion • *Adjective:* concluding

Word Partners	
• reasonably _____	If you came to class in the morning and no one was there, you could **reasonably conclude** that you were early for school.

Verbal Practice

Talk about It   **Read** each sentence and **think** about how you would complete it.

           Discuss your idea with your partner using the sentence frame.

           Listen carefully to your partner's and classmates' ideas.

           Write your favorite idea in the blank.

❶ My best friend and I often **conclude** our phone conversations by saying,

     "_____ ."

❷ Our gym teacher usually **concludes** class by _____ .

❸ When the principal suddenly announced on the loudspeaker that everyone had to exit the building, we **concluded** that _____ .

❹ If you walked into a room and everybody was laughing, you might **conclude** that

     _____ .

conclude
verb

Writing Practice

Collaborate **Work with your partner** to complete the sentence using the correct form of **conclude** and appropriate content.

Hundreds of years ago, astronomers incorrectly _____ that the Earth was

_____ .

Your Turn **Work independently** to complete the sentence using the correct form of **conclude** and appropriate content.

If an entire class got poor grades on a _____ , the teacher might

_____ that _____ .

Be an Academic Author **Work independently** to write two sentences using Meaning 2 of **conclude**. In your first sentence, use **conclude** with the modal verb *might*. In your second sentence, use **conclude** in the *simple past tense*.

❶ _____

_____

❷ _____

_____

grammar tip

Modal verbs are helping verbs that give additional meaning to the main verb. *Might* can be used to express possibility.

If you saw a baby crying, you **might conclude** that he was hungry.

She **might meet** us later.

Write an Academic Paragraph **Complete** the paragraph using the correct form of **conclude** and original content.

The Civil War, which began in 1861 and _____ ❶ in 1865, was the deadliest

war ever fought in the United States. In the 1800s, Southern states relied on slaves to work on their

_____ ❷ . When Abraham Lincoln was _____ ❸

president in 1860, Southern states were _____ ❹ about the future of slavery

because Lincoln opposed it. In a famous speech, Lincoln _____ ❺ that

slavery was immoral, which upset many Southern slave owners. As a result of Lincoln's views,

in 1861, 11 Southern states seceded from the United States. This triggered the start of the Civil War

and resulted in four years of bloody _____ ❻ and the deaths of 620,000

soldiers. After the war ended, Americans eventually came to _____ ❼ that

slavery was immoral, and it was outlawed in the United States.

conclusion

noun

▶ **Say it:** con • **clu** • sion   **Write it:** _____

Academic Vocabulary Toolkit

Meanings	Examples
1. the end of something *Synonyms:* ending, finish	1. The _____ ceremony marked the **conclusion** of the _____ .
2. a decision you make *Synonym:* judgment	2. In the robbery case, the _____ reached the **conclusion** that the defendant was _____ .

Forms	Family
• *Singular:* conclusion • *Plural:* conclusions	• *Verb:* conclude • *Adjective:* concluding

Word Partners	
• come to the ____ that	The band **came to the conclusion that** they should do a carwash for their yearly fundraiser.
• draw the ____ that	When Samantha didn't come to school for two days, we **drew the conclusion that** she was sick.

Verbal Practice

Talk about It **Read** each sentence and **think** about how you would complete it.

Discuss your idea with your partner using the sentence frame.

Listen carefully to your partner's and classmates' ideas.

Write your favorite idea in the blank.

❶ When you write an essay, it's important to include _____ and a strong **conclusion**.

❷ Each school year comes to a **conclusion** with _____ .

❸ If I met someone who was mean to people all of the time, I would probably draw the **conclusion** that he or she _____ .

❹ After searching for my phone, I reached the **conclusion** that I had

_____ .

Writing Practice

Collaborate   **Work with your partner** to complete the sentence using the correct form of **conclusion** and appropriate content.

My friend and I drew different _____ about who should

_____ .

Your Turn   **Work independently** to complete the sentence using the correct form of **conclusion** and appropriate content.

If you saw one of your classmates crying, you might come to the _____

that _____ .

Be an Academic Author   **Work independently** to write two sentences using Meaning 2 of **conclusion**. In your first sentence, use **conclusion** in the *singular form*. In your second sentence, use **conclusion** in the *plural form*.

❶ _____

_____

❷ _____

_____

grammar tip

Count nouns name things that can be counted. Count nouns have two forms, singular and plural. To make most count nouns plural, add *–s*.

We came to different conclusions.

He likes board games.

Write an Academic Paragraph   **Complete** the paragraph using the correct form of **conclusion** and original content.

The scientific method has four _____ : observation, hypothesis,
                ❶

testing, and conclusion. First, a researcher observes a _____ and takes
                ❷

notes about it. Next, he or she forms a hypothesis that attempts to _____
                ❸

the phenomenon he or she has observed. During the third step, testing, the researcher

_____ experiments that test his or her hypothesis. If the experiment
        ❹

proves the hypothesis wrong, the researcher must start over because there is no evidence from

which he or she can draw a _____ . However, if the experiment supports
           ❺

the researcher's hypothesis, he or she can reach a _____ based on the
           ❻

results. The researcher can then publish the _____ in scientific journals.
           ❼

consequence
noun

Say it: **con** · se · quence   Write it: _____

<table>
<tr><th>Meaning</th><th colspan="2">Example</th></tr>
<tr><td>the result of something that happens

Synonym: outcome</td><td colspan="2">If you leave your bedroom _____ open when it rains, the **consequence** is that your belongings get _____ .</td></tr>
</table>

Academic Vocabulary Toolkit

Forms	Family
• **Singular:** consequence • **Plural:** consequences	• **Adjective:** consequent • **Adverb:** consequently

Word Partners

• direct _____	Hannah's bad grades were a **direct consequence** of her poor study habits.
• negative _____	One **negative consequence** of a snowstorm is that you might not be able to leave your house.
• suffer the _____ s	When Jake played basketball without stretching first, he **suffered the consequences**.

Verbal Practice

Talk about It   **Read** each sentence and **think** about how you would complete it.

Discuss your idea with your partner using the sentence frame.

Listen carefully to your partner's and classmates' ideas.

Write your favorite idea in the blank.

❶ If I oversleep on a school day, the **consequence** is that I _____ .

❷ If you do something bad like _____ , you must be ready to pay the **consequences**.

48

Writing Practice

Collaborate **Work with your partner** to complete the sentence using the correct form of **consequence** and appropriate content.

One _____ of volunteering is that it makes you feel good about

_____ .

Your Turn **Work independently** to complete the sentence using the correct form of **consequence** and appropriate content.

If I disrespected my teacher or principal, I would probably suffer the _____

because _____ .

Be an Academic Author **Work independently** to write two sentences. In your first sentence, use **consequence** in the *singular form* and include a word partner. In your second sentence, use **consequence** in the *plural form*.

❶ _____

_____

❷ _____

_____

Write an Academic Paragraph **Complete** the paragraph using the correct form of **consequence** and original content.

In life, every action has a consequence, but not all _____ ❶

carry the same importance. For example, some consequences are minor, like having to

make up a _____ ❷ after missing class or getting grounded for

_____ ❸ . Other consequences are slightly more significant;

for example, if you _____ ❹ with a friend, you may not speak to each other

for a short period of time. However, some consequences are very _____ ❺

and can impact your life for a long time. For instance, the _____ ❻ of

stealing may involve getting arrested, paying a fine, and sometimes even going to jail. It is

important to consider the _____ ❼ of all of your actions and think before

you _____ ❽ .

consequently
adverb

Academic Vocabulary Toolkit

Meaning	Example	
as a result of something *Synonym:* accordingly	There have been a number of _____ on Chestnut Street recently; **consequently**, the _____ have been patrolling the area.	

Family

• *Noun:* consequence

Verbal Practice

Talk about It **Read** each sentence and **think** about how you would complete it.

Discuss your idea with your partner using the sentence frame.

Listen carefully to your partner's and classmates' ideas.

Write your favorite idea in the blank.

❶ The principal quickly discovered which students had glued all the lockers shut. **Consequently**, he called those students into his office and

_____ .

❷ We stayed up until midnight watching _____ ;

consequently, we were very tired the next day.

Writing Practice

Collaborate **Work with your partner** to complete the sentence using **consequently** and appropriate content.

Each year large amounts of pollution are released into the Earth's oceans. _____ ,

there are now problems such as _____ .

Your Turn **Work independently** to complete the sentences using **consequently** and appropriate content.

My goal for this year is to _____ . _____ , I have

been working hard and _____ .

Be an **Work independently** to write two sentences. In your first sentence, use **consequently** with a
Academic verb in the *simple past tense*. In your second sentence, use **consequently** with a verb in the *simple*
Author *present tense*.

❶ _____

_____

❷ _____

_____

> ## grammar tip
>
> *Consequently* **is an adverb that acts as a conjunction. It is often used with a semicolon to connect two independent clauses.**
>
> It was raining hard; **consequently**, we stayed inside.

Write an **Complete** the paragraph using **consequently** and original content.
Academic
Paragraph "Generation gap" is a term used to _____ a phenomenon
                                                    ❶

affecting older and younger generations who have grown up in different circumstances

and, _____ , sometimes have trouble understanding each
           ❷

other. One contribution to generation gaps that exist today is the rapid development

of technology in the past few decades. For example, many teenagers know more about

_____ and surfing the Internet than their older relatives. Older
         ❸

generations sometimes don't see the appeal of _____ or the Internet;
                                                          ❹

_____ , they don't understand why younger generations spend so much
         ❺

time using them. Generation gaps sometimes cause _____ between
                                                              ❻

younger and older people, but each generation has valuable advice to share with the other about

love, work, and _____ .
                     ❼

51

consider
verb

▶ **Say it:** con • **si** • der   **Write it:** _____

Academic Vocabulary Toolkit

Meanings	Examples	
1. to think about something carefully *Synonym:* reflect	**1.** Sara **considered** getting a _____ for lunch, but then she decided to order a healthy _____ instead.	
2. to have an opinion about something *Synonyms:* think, believe	**2.** Teenagers often **consider** their parents' taste in _____ to be old-fashioned or _____ .	

Forms		Family
Present: I/You/We/They consider He/She/It considers **Past:** considered		• **Noun:** consideration

Word Partners	
• carefully _____	Before you act, you should **carefully consider** the consequences.
• _____ the possibilities	If you **consider the possibilities** of life in space, it seems likely that we are not alone in the universe.

Verbal Practice

Talk about It **Read** each sentence and **think** about how you would complete it.

Discuss your idea with your partner using the sentence frame.

Listen carefully to your partner's and classmates' ideas.

Write your favorite idea in the blank.

❶ Nina **considered** buying her brother a _____ .

❷ Before you enroll in a class, you should **consider** _____ .

❸ I **consider** _____ to be the best show on TV.

❹ Who do you **consider** to be the better singer: _____ or _____ ?

Writing Practice

Collaborate **Work with your partner** to complete the sentences using the correct form of **consider** and appropriate content.

❶ If you are _____ going to college, you should do some research online and

find out _____ .

❷ Many students _____ summer camp to be _____ .

Your Turn **Work independently** to complete the sentences using the correct form of **consider** and appropriate content.

❶ Last weekend, I _____ going to _____ with my friends,

but we went to _____ instead.

❷ I would _____ a B+ to be a good grade in _____ .

Be an Academic Author **Work independently** to write two sentences. In your first sentence, use **consider** in the *simple past tense*. In your second sentence, use **consider** in the *simple present tense*.

MEANING ❶ _____

_____

MEANING ❷ _____

_____

> **grammar tip**
>
> To make the simple past tense of regular verbs, add –*ed* or –*d*.
>
> Mike consider**ed** getting a job.
>
> She chang**ed** her answer.

Write an Academic Paragraph **Complete** the paragraph using the correct form of **consider** and original content.

Many young people have role models—someone they _____ ❶ and

admire. However, sometimes parents and teachers do not _____ ❷

certain role models to be appropriate choices for kids. For example, celebrities such as

_____ ❸ or professional athletes like _____ ❹

have achieved many professional accomplishments, but they have also made mistakes in their

personal lives. Parents and teachers argue that people who have _____ ❺

are not acceptable role models. One idea to _____ ❻ , however, is that

everyone makes mistakes—and kids can still _____ ❼ someone without

wanting to be exactly like them.

53

contrast
verb

▶ *Say it:*   con • **trast**   *Write it:* _____

<table>
<tr><th colspan="2">Meaning</th><th colspan="2">Example</th></tr>
</table>

Meaning	Example
to show how two things are different	You can **contrast** oranges and lemons by saying that oranges are _____ and lemons are _____ .

Academic Vocabulary Toolkit

Forms		Family
Present:		• **Noun:** contrast
I/You/We/They	contrast	• **Adjective:** contrasting
He/She/It	contrasts	
Past:	contrasted	

Word Partners

• compare and _____	I am going to **compare and contrast** ice cream and frozen yogurt for my health class essay.

Verbal Practice

Talk about It   **Read** each sentence and **think** about how you would complete it.

Discuss your idea with your partner using the sentence frame.

Listen carefully to your partner's and classmates' ideas.

Write your favorite idea in the blank.

❶ Teachers often ask students to compare and **contrast** two different

_____ in a story.

❷ If you **contrasted** the typical school day of a kindergartener with someone in high

school, one major difference would be that _____ .

Writing Practice

Collaborate **Work with your partner** to complete the sentence using the correct form of **contrast** and appropriate content.

If you _____ life in the United States with life in _____ ,

you might say that in the U.S. people tend to _____ more.

Your Turn **Work independently** to complete the sentence using the correct form of **contrast** and appropriate content.

In my last English paper, I _____ the two characters _____ and

_____ .

Be an Academic Author **Work independently** to write two sentences. In your first sentence, use **contrast** in the *simple past tense*. In your second sentence, use **contrast** with the word partner *compare and contrast*.

❶ _____

_____

❷ _____

_____

> **grammar tip**
>
> **To make the simple past tense of regular verbs, add –ed or –d.**
>
> She contrast**ed** two poems for her essay.
>
> He chang**ed** his answer.

Write an Academic Paragraph **Complete** the paragraph using the correct form of **contrast** and original content.

Compare and _____❶ papers are common assignments in school. In

these papers, students describe the similarities and _____❷ between two

things. Students might contrast two places, such as Mexico and _____❸ ,

two people, such as President Obama and _____❹ , or even two time

periods. For example, in a history class, a teacher may ask students to _____❺

life in a different century with life in the present. When writing these papers, it's a good idea

to choose two things that have a number of attributes in common but also many different

_____❻ as well. For example, bus travel and air travel can be compared

and _____❼ because they are both methods of transportation, though

one is much faster than the other.

contribute
verb

Say it: con • **trib** • ute

Write it: _____

Academic Vocabulary Toolkit

Meanings	Examples
1. to give money or resources to something *Synonym:* donate	1. Each _____ **contributed** one can of _____ for the food drive at school.
2. to participate in a group by saying or doing something	2. Teachers expect _____ to **contribute** to class by _____ in discussions.

Forms	Family
Present: I/You/We/They contribute He/She/It contributes **Past:** contributed	• **Noun:** contribution

Word Partners

• _____ to the development of something   Hormones **contribute to the development** of every human being.

Verbal Practice

Talk about It   **Read** each sentence and **think** about how you would complete it.

Discuss your idea with your partner using the sentence frame.

Listen carefully to your partner's and classmates' ideas.

Write your favorite idea in the blank.

❶ It's helpful when people **contribute** items such as _____ to homeless shelters.

❷ In the past, my family has **contributed** _____ to people in need.

❸ In a group project, students can **contribute** in a variety of ways, such as by _____ .

❹ Our class could **contribute** to the local community by _____ .

Writing Practice

Collaborate **Work with your partner** to complete the sentence using the correct form of **contribute** and appropriate content.

Some students don't like to _____ in class because they

_____ .

Your Turn **Work independently** to complete the sentence using the correct form of **contribute** and appropriate content.

One group that I have _____ to in my school or community is

_____ , where I _____ .

Be an Academic Author **Work independently** to write two sentences using Meaning 2 of **contribute**. In your first sentence, use **contribute** in the *simple present tense*. In your second sentence, use **contribute** in the *present perfect tense*.

❶ _____

_____

❷ _____

_____

> ### grammar tip
>
> **The present perfect tense is formed with *has/have* + the past participle form of the verb. To make the past participle of regular verbs, add *–ed* or *–d*.**
>
> She <u>has contributed</u> her ideas to the project.
>
> I <u>have received</u> a letter.

Write an Academic Paragraph **Complete** the paragraph using the correct form of **contribute** and original content.

People often wonder whether happiness can be measured.

For instance, is happiness how many _____ a person has or how
                                              ❶

much money he or she makes? Studies suggest that people are actually happiest when they

_____ to a group. Whether they're rich or poor, people like to feel
        ❷

that they are _____ something larger than themselves. For example,
                      ❸

many people enjoy _____ to groups that do charitable work, such
                            ❹

as _____ . Other people work with their neighbors and plan ways
       ❺

to _____ to neighborhood improvements, such as picking up litter.
      ❻

Joining a _____ in your community can help you meet more people
                ❼

and discover ways to make contributions to your neighborhood.

contribution
noun

▶ **Say it:** con • tri • **bu** • tion   **Write it:** _____

Academic Vocabulary Toolkit

Meanings	Examples	
1. money or resources you give to something *Synonym:* donation	**1.** Everyone made a **contribution** of _____ dollars to buy Sam a birthday _____ .	
2. something you do or say to help others	**2.** Mike's **contributions** on the _____ field helped his team _____ the game.	

Forms	Family
• *Singular:* contribution • *Plural:* contributions	• *Verb:* contribute

Word Partners	
• important ____	The light bulb was an **important contribution** to technology.
• major ____	Rosa Parks made a **major contribution** to the civil rights movement.
• significant ____	I hope to make a **significant contribution** to the field of architecture someday.

Verbal Practice

Talk about It **Read** each sentence and **think** about how you would complete it.

Discuss your idea with your partner using the sentence frame.

Listen carefully to your partner's and classmates' ideas.

Write your favorite idea in the blank.

❶ Animal shelters rely on **contributions** of items such as _____ .

❷ Students at our school recently collected **contributions** for

_____ .

❸ School newspapers often feature **contributions** by students about topics like

_____ .

❹ _____ has made many **contributions** to world peace.

Writing Practice

Collaborate   **Work with your partner** to complete the sentence using the correct form of **contribution** and appropriate content.

Some streets in this neighborhood, such as _____ , are named after

people who have made significant _____ to our community.

Your Turn   **Work independently** to complete the sentence using the correct form of **contribution** and appropriate content.

I think that _____ has made an important _____

to the field of _____ .

Be an Academic Author   **Work independently** to write two sentences using Meaning 2 of **contribution**. In your first sentence, use **contribution** in the *plural form* with the quantifier *many*. In your second sentence, use **contribution** in the *singular form* and include a word partner.

❶ _____

_____

❷ _____

_____

> ## grammar tip
>
> Quantifiers are words that tell us how much or how many of something there is. They usually come before the noun they describe.
>
> She has made **many** contributions to our team.
>
> He has a **few** ideas.

Write an Academic Paragraph   **Complete** the paragraph using the correct form of **contribution** and original content.

       Many people feel that social networking Web sites like Facebook and

_____ have made significant _____ to the way
             ❶   ❷

people communicate. These Web sites make it possible to _____ with
                                                          ❸

friends and family members all over the world. However, some people argue that social networking

Web sites also _____ to a number of problems for Internet users. One
                      ❹

concern is that these Web sites facilitate _____ like cyber bullying and
                                               ❺

online stalking. Another concern is that these Web sites encourage people to spend more time

_____ with people over the computer than face-to-face. Nevertheless,
            ❻

while these are legitimate concerns, there is no doubt that social networking Web sites are valuable

_____ to the way people stay in touch today.
            ❼

convince
verb

Academic Vocabulary Toolkit

Meaning	Example	
to persuade someone to do or believe something	At first Ian didn't want to go _____ , but we finally **convinced** him to jump in the _____ .	

Forms		Family
Present:		• *Adjective:* convincing
I/You/We/They	convince	
He/She/It	convinces	
Past:	convinced	

Word Partners

• manage to _____ someone	Emma **managed to convince** her little sister that the tooth fairy was real.
• try to _____ someone	Paul **tried to convince** his friend Molly that he saw a UFO, but she didn't believe him.

Verbal Practice

Talk about It **Read** each sentence and **think** about how you would complete it.

Discuss your idea with your partner using the sentence frame.

Listen carefully to your partner's and classmates' ideas.

Write your favorite idea in the blank.

❶ Last weekend my friend **convinced** me to go to

_____ .

❷ If someone started a rumor about me, I would try to **convince** everyone

that _____ .

Writing Practice

Collaborate   **Work with your partner** to complete the sentence using the correct form of **convince** and appropriate content.

Our class will try to _____ our teacher that we should go on a field trip

to _____ .

Your Turn   **Work independently** to complete the sentence using the correct form of **convince** and appropriate content.

You could never _____ me to believe that _____ .

Be an Academic Author   **Work independently** to write two sentences. In your first sentence, use **convince** in the *simple past tense*. In your second sentence, use **convince** with the modal verb *will*.

❶ _____

_____

❷ _____

_____

> ### grammar tip
>
> **Modal verbs are helping verbs that give additional meaning to the main verb. *Will* can be used to express a prediction.**
>
> I **will** convince Jamal to come with us.
>
> They **will** win this game.

Write an Academic Paragraph   **Complete** the paragraph using the correct form of **convince** and original content.

Psychologists have determined that there are a number of clues people can use to

_____ whether someone is telling a lie. First, look at the person's eyes
      ❶

while they are speaking to you. People who are lying often have _____
      ❷

making eye contact. Some people, however, are aware of this tendency and will actually

maintain intense eye contact in order to _____ you that their story
      ❸

is true! Second, listen to the person's voice. People tend to _____ at
      ❹

a higher pitch when they lie. Finally, _____ the content of the story
      ❺

itself for any irregularities. If you ask the person for more information, they may have trouble

_____ you small details. These clues may help you realize if someone is
      ❻

lying to you—even if they try to _____ you otherwise.
      ❼

convincing
adjective

Academic Vocabulary Toolkit

Meaning	Example
making you believe something	Kara didn't think that Sid's
Antonym: unconvincing	_____ for missing their _____ was very **convincing**.

Family

- **Verb:** convince
- **Adverb:** convincingly

Word Partners

- _____ argument   When you write a persuasive essay, the first thing you need is a **convincing argument**.

- _____ evidence   The prosecutor lacked **convincing evidence**, so the jury let the defendant go free.

- _____ explanation   Mr. Trakas gave a **convincing explanation** of how caterpillars become butterflies.

Verbal Practice

Talk about It **Read** each sentence and **think** about how you would complete it.

Discuss your idea with your partner using the sentence frame.

Listen carefully to your partner's and classmates' ideas.

Write your favorite idea in the blank.

❶ "_____" is not a **convincing** explanation for failing to turn in your homework.

❷ I think that _____ gave a very **convincing** performance in the movie _____ .

Writing Practice

Collaborate   **Work with your partner** to complete the sentence using **convincing** and appropriate content.

The most _____ explanation for why people have different personalities is

that _____ .

Your Turn   **Work independently** to complete the sentence using **convincing** and appropriate content.

One _____ argument for owning an MP3 player is that

_____ .

Be an Academic Author   **Work independently** to write two sentences. In your first sentence, use **convincing** with a *plural noun*. In your second sentence, use **convincing** with the word partner *convincing explanation*.

❶ _____

_____

❷ _____

_____

> ### grammar tip
>
> **Adjectives do not have plural forms. Do not add an –s to adjectives when they describe plural nouns.**
>
> <u>convincing</u> arguments
>
> <u>loud</u> dogs

Write an Academic Paragraph   **Complete** the paragraph using **convincing** and original content.

Joining your school's debate team can help you develop many valuable

_____ both inside and outside of the classroom. First of all,
        ❶

you will improve your ability to make _____ arguments for and
                                              ❷

against many topics because debating requires you to examine an issue from many

_____ in order to thoroughly understand it. Second, you will learn
        ❸

to work effectively with a team to brainstorm ideas and solve _____ .
                                                                      ❹

Third, you will improve your public speaking abilities and gain _____
                                                                        ❺

performing in front of an audience. All of these skills are useful in the classroom as well as in

professional _____ later in your life. If you are able to clearly articulate
                    ❻

your opinions and present _____ ideas, you will certainly become
                                ❼

a leader in whichever field you choose.

define
verb

Academic Vocabulary Toolkit

Meaning	Example	Periods of time
to explain the meaning of a word or concept	A _____ dictionary **defines** words using detailed _____ and illustrations.	a minute an hour

Forms		Family
Present: I/You/We/They define He/She/It defines		• **Noun:** definition
Past: defined		• **Adjective:** defined

Word Partners

• clearly _____   The law **clearly defines** a minor as someone who is under 18.

Verbal Practice

Talk about It   **Read** each sentence and **think** about how you would complete it.

Discuss your idea with your partner using the sentence frame.

Listen carefully to your partner's and classmates' ideas.

Write your favorite idea in the blank.

❶ I would **define** a good leader as someone who _____ .

❷ Today we **define** a celebrity as anyone who _____ .

Writing Practice

Collaborate **Work with your partner** to complete the sentence using the correct form of **define** and appropriate content.

The dictionary _____ the word "_____" as meaning

"_____."

Your Turn **Work independently** to complete the sentence using the correct form of **define** and appropriate content.

I would _____ a good vacation as one in which I get the chance to

_____ .

Be an Academic Author **Work independently** to write two sentences. In your first sentence, use **define** with the modal verb *would*. In your second sentence, use **define** in the *simple present tense*.

❶ _____

_____

❷ _____

_____

> ### grammar tip
>
> Modal verbs are helping verbs that give additional meaning to the main verb. *Would* can be used to express a preference.
>
> I **would** **define** my style as sporty.
>
> We **would** **like** some water.

Write an Academic Paragraph **Complete** the paragraph using the correct form of **define** and original content.

Thomas Edison _____ ❶ genius as one percent inspiration and ninety-

nine percent perspiration. Inventors in all fields—art, science, _____ ❷ ,

and more—must have the patience and drive to turn their ideas into reality. For example,

musicians may have natural _____ ❸ , but they still have to study and

_____ ❹ for years in order to master their craft. Writers may have a brilliant

idea for a screenplay or _____ ❺ , but they typically spend long hours

brainstorming and _____ ❻ on the computer. While some people would

argue that what truly _____ ❼ a genius is their inspiration and ideas, there

is no denying that no idea can come to reality without plenty of hard work (or perspiration).

demonstrate
verb

Academic Vocabulary Toolkit

Meanings	Examples
1. to show someone how to do something **Synonym:** explain	**1.** Julia **demonstrated** her ability to _____ for the talent show.
2. to show that something is true	**2.** Studies **demonstrate** that drinking _____ can contribute to _____ .

Forms	Family
Present: I/You/We/They demonstrate He/She/It demonstrates **Past:** demonstrated	• **Noun:** demonstration • **Adjective:** demonstrative

Word Partners

- _____ (my/your/his/her/our/their) ability
- studies _____ that

Ralph **demonstrated his ability** to do a cartwheel during gym class.

Studies demonstrate that drinking at least four glasses of water a day has significant health benefits.

Verbal Practice

Talk about It **Read** each sentence and **think** about how you would complete it.

Discuss your idea with your partner using the sentence frame.

Listen carefully to your partner's and classmates' ideas.

Write your favorite idea in the blank.

❶ Last week our teacher **demonstrated** how to _____ .

❷ Most teenagers could **demonstrate** how to _____ .

❸ Frequently coming late to class **demonstrates** that you need to

_____ .

❹ Research **demonstrates** that too much sun exposure causes

_____ .

Writing Practice

Collaborate | **Work with your partner** to complete the sentence using the correct form of **demonstrate** and appropriate content.

A lot of trophies and awards in someone's living room might _____ that he or

she is an excellent _____ .

Your Turn | **Work independently** to complete the sentence using the word **demonstrate** and appropriate content.

Studies have _____ that drinking a lot of caffeine can cause you to

_____ .

Be an Academic Author | **Work independently** to write two sentences using Meaning 2 of **demonstrate**. In your first sentence, use **demonstrate** in the *simple present tense*. In your second sentence, use **demonstrate** in the *present perfect tense*.

❶ _____

_____

❷ _____

_____

grammar tip

The present perfect tense is formed with *has/have* + the past participle form of the verb. To make the past participle of regular verbs, add *–ed* or *–d*.

She <u>has demonstrated</u> her desire to win.

We <u>have played</u> this game before.

Write an Academic Paragraph | **Complete** the paragraph using the correct form of **demonstrate** and original content.

In recent years, funding for community art programs has decreased even though

numerous studies have _____ that art programs provide many

❶

_____ for young people and adults. First of all, art classes

❷

help people _____ themselves creatively and understand

❸

other _____ and perspectives. Additionally, research

❹

_____ that young people who participate in art programs are less likely

❺

to engage in destructive activities such as _____ . Elderly individuals

❻

can also improve their motor coordination by regularly _____ in artistic

❼

activities. Art programs serve an _____ function in communities and

❽

may become endangered if funding cuts continue.

demonstration
noun

Academic Vocabulary Toolkit

Meaning	Example
a display or explanation of something **Synonym:** presentation	The _____ employee gave a **demonstration** on how to properly use a life _____ .

Forms	Family
• **Singular:** demonstration • **Plural:** demonstrations	• **Verb:** demonstrate • **Adjective:** demonstrative

Word Partners	
• give a _____	Our chemistry teacher **gave a demonstration** on how to safely handle chemicals.

Verbal Practice

Talk about It   **Read** each sentence and **think** about how you would complete it.

Discuss your idea with your partner using the sentence frame.

Listen carefully to your partner's and classmates' ideas.

Write your favorite idea in the blank.

❶ You can go online and find video **demonstrations** on how to play

_____ .

❷ A survival expert could give a **demonstration** on how to

_____ .

Writing Practice

Collaborate **Work with your partner** to complete the sentence using the correct form of **demonstration** and appropriate content.

It is important to pay close attention to safety _____ on how to

_____ so you know what to do in an emergency.

Your Turn **Work independently** to complete the sentence using the correct form of **demonstration** and appropriate content.

One of the most interesting _____ that I have seen on TV was how to

_____ .

Be an Academic Author **Work independently** to write two sentences. In your first sentence, use **demonstration** in the *singular form*. In your second sentence, use **demonstration** in the *plural form*.

❶ _____

_____

❷ _____

_____

grammar tip

Count nouns name things that can be counted. Count nouns have two forms, singular and plural. To make most count nouns plural, add –s.

Our science teacher often gives demonstrations in class.

He likes board games.

Write an Academic Paragraph **Complete** the paragraph using the correct form of **demonstration** and original content.

One important safety _____❶_____ you should see is CPR, or

cardiopulmonary resuscitation. CPR is given to _____❷_____ who are suffering

cardiac arrest or have stopped breathing. A CPR _____❸_____ involves

using a mannequin in order to show how to perform CPR on a real person. The teacher will

demonstrate how to _____❹_____ chest compressions with your hands and

breathe into a person's mouth in order to help them _____❺_____ . CPR is

_____❻_____ for restoring oxygen to a person's heart and brain so they don't

die. In just a few short hours, you can _____❼_____ CPR and help someone

in a life-threatening emergency.

describe
verb

Academic Vocabulary Toolkit

Meaning	Example	
to say what someone or something is like	Chris lovingly **described** his new _____ to me over the _____ .	

Forms		Family
Present:		• **Noun:** description
I/You/We/They	describe	• **Adjective:** descriptive
He/She/It	describes	• **Adverb:** descriptively
Past:	described	

Word Partners

• accurately _____	You could **accurately describe** Michael Jordan as a basketball legend.
• _____ something in detail	The newspaper article **described the tragedy in detail**.

Verbal Practice

Talk about It **Read** each sentence and **think** about how you would complete it.

Discuss your idea with your partner using the sentence frame.

Listen carefully to your partner's and classmates' ideas.

Write your favorite idea in the blank.

❶ I would **describe** my best friend as someone who is _____ .

❷ My family often **describes** me as a _____ person.

Writing Practice

Collaborate **Work with your partner** to complete the sentence using the correct form of **describe** and appropriate content.

In the novel _____ , the author _____ the lives of characters

such as _____ in detail.

Your Turn **Work independently** to complete the sentence using the correct form of **describe** and appropriate content.

I would _____ the performer _____ as

_____ and extremely _____ .

Be an Academic Author **Work independently** to write two sentences. In your first sentence, use **describe** with the modal verb *would*. In your second sentence, use **describe** in the *simple present tense*.

❶ _____

_____

❷ _____

_____

> ### grammar tip
>
> Modal verbs are helping verbs that give additional meaning to the main verb. *Would* can be used to express a preference.
>
> I **would** describe myself as organized.
>
> He **would like** to meet her.

Write an Academic Paragraph **Complete** the paragraph using the correct form of **describe** and original content.

Whether you're writing fiction or _____ , the language you use
❶

to _____ the setting, characters, and _____
❷ ❸

of a story can make all the difference between a dull, _____ text and
❹

a vibrant, exciting one. Using descriptive adjectives such as "_____"
❺

will make your readers feel like they are watching the story unfold right in front of them.

For example, "The girl sat on the floor of the room" is far less interesting to imagine than

"The _____ , freckled girl sat on the gleaming wood floor in the middle
❻

of the vast, empty room." The more precise and colorful that your descriptions are, the more

_____ the reader will become, and the more fun you'll have while writing.
❼

description
noun

Say it: de • **scrip** • tion   *Write it:* _____

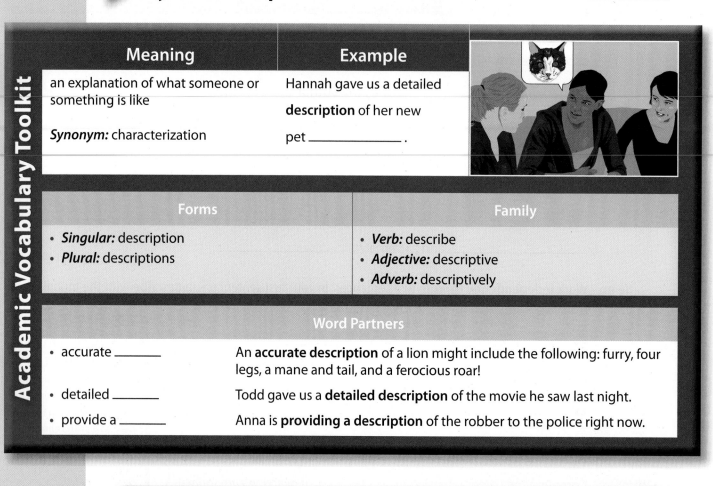

Meaning	Example
an explanation of what someone or something is like *Synonym:* characterization	Hannah gave us a detailed **description** of her new pet _____ .

Forms	Family
• *Singular:* description • *Plural:* descriptions	• *Verb:* describe • *Adjective:* descriptive • *Adverb:* descriptively

Word Partners	
• accurate _____	An **accurate description** of a lion might include the following: furry, four legs, a mane and tail, and a ferocious roar!
• detailed _____	Todd gave us a **detailed description** of the movie he saw last night.
• provide a _____	Anna is **providing a description** of the robber to the police right now.

Verbal Practice

Talk about It   **Read** each sentence and **think** about how you would complete it.

Discuss your idea with your partner using the sentence frame.

Listen carefully to your partner's and classmates' ideas.

Write your favorite idea in the blank.

❶ If I had to provide a **description** of my classmates, I would say that they are

_____ .

❷ I just read a brief **description** of a really interesting movie called

_____ on the Web site _____ .

Writing Practice

Collaborate **Work with your partner** to complete the sentence using the correct form of **description** and appropriate content.

On our last _____ test, we had to write a detailed _____ of

_____ .

Your Turn **Work independently** to complete the sentence using the correct form of **description** and appropriate content.

If I had to give an accurate _____ of my school, I would say that it

has _____ and is painted _____ .

Be an Academic Author **Work independently** to write two sentences. In your first sentence, use **description** in the *singular form* and include a word partner. In your second sentence, use **description** in the *plural form*.

❶ _____

_____

❷ _____

_____

> ### grammar tip
> Count nouns name things that can be counted. Count nouns have two forms, singular and plural. To make most count nouns plural, add –*s*.
>
> My descriptions were inaccurate.
>
> He likes board games.

Write an Academic Paragraph **Complete** the paragraph using the correct form of **description** and original content.

Police sketch artists have a very _____ role in law enforcement. ❶

These professionals use their artistic _____ to help police catch people ❷

suspected of committing _____ . A police sketch artist draws a suspect ❸

based on the physical _____ given by a witness or victim of a crime. It's a ❹

challenging _____ because the artist needs not only the ability to draw ❺

well but also the sensitivity and patience to elicit an accurate _____ ❻

from someone who may be emotionally traumatized or upset. If you think you might be

interested in becoming a police sketch artist, start taking classes in art and psychology,

and practice drawing _____ . Your artistic skills could one day ❼

help _____ . ❽

develop
verb

▶ *Say it:* de • **vel** • op   *Write it:* _____

Meanings	Examples	
1. to begin to happen *Synonym:* start	**1.** A flood **developed** after several days of _____ .	
2. to change into something bigger, stronger, or more advanced *Synonym:* grow	**2.** A young boy will eventually **develop** into a grown _____ .	

Forms		Family
Present: I/You/We/They develop He/She/It develops **Past:** developed		• **Noun:** development • **Adjectives:** developed, developing, developmental

Word Partners	
• _____ skills	An internship can help you **develop skills** in the workplace.
• _____ the ability to do something	After a lot of practice, I **developed the ability to** walk on my hands.
• help _____	Running **helps develop** endurance and muscle mass.

Verbal Practice

Talk about It   **Read** each sentence and **think** about how you would complete it.

                Discuss your idea with your partner using the sentence frame.

                Listen carefully to your partner's and classmates' ideas.

                Write your favorite idea in the blank.

❶ After Kevin stayed out in the snow for several hours, he **developed**

     _____ .

❷ _____ is a problem that can **develop** at school if students

     don't do anything about it.

❸ I lift weights and exercise to **develop** _____ .

❹ If you work hard, you can **develop** the ability to _____ .

Writing Practice

Collaborate   **Work with your partner** to complete the sentences using the correct form of **develop** and appropriate content.

❶ The best way to handle a disagreement that has _____ in class is to

_____ .

❷ In the future, scientists will probably _____ technology that allows people

_____ .

Your Turn   **Work independently** to complete the sentences using the correct form of **develop** and appropriate content.

❶ A problem _____ between my _____ and me when

_____ .

❷ Over the past year, I have _____ my _____ skills.

Be an Academic Author   **Work independently** to write two sentences. In your first sentence, use **develop** in the *simple past tense*. In your second sentence, use **develop** in the *present perfect tense.*

MEANING ❶ _____

_____

MEANING ❷ _____

_____

> ### grammar tip
>
> **The present perfect tense is formed with *has/have* + the past participle form of the verb. To make the past participle of regular verbs, add *–ed* or *–d*.**
>
> She <u>has develop**ed**</u> her acting skills in the last year.
>
> You <u>have received</u> a letter.

Write an Academic Paragraph   **Complete** the paragraph using the correct form of **develop** and original content.

When you _____ from a _____ into an
      ❶   ❷

adolescent, and eventually an adult, every year is physically different than the year before. Compare

yourself now to how you were five years ago. Can you _____ faster
           ❸

and lift heavier objects? Over time, your muscles and bones _____ ,
           ❹

making you stronger. Another important part of your _____ also
           ❺

developed—your brain. For instance, you are now able to have articulate conversations about

_____ topics because your brain grew and _____
      ❻   ❼

with the rest of your body.

development
noun

Say it: de • **vel** • op • ment   **Write it:** _____

Academic Vocabulary Toolkit

Meanings	Examples
1. the growth or progress of something	1. The weather _____ is tracking the **development** of a major _____ .
2. an event that changes a situation **Synonym:** change	2. The _____ on TV lets us know about recent **developments** in a _____ .

Forms	Family
• *Singular:* development • *Plural:* developments	• *Verb:* develop • *Adjectives:* developed, developing, developmental

Word Partners
• stage of _____   An egg is the first **stage of development** in the life of a frog.

Verbal Practice

Talk about It   **Read** each sentence and **think** about how you would complete it.

Discuss your idea with your partner using the sentence frame.

Listen carefully to your partner's and classmates' ideas.

Write your favorite idea in the blank.

❶ To encourage the **development** of children in school, parents and teachers should

_____ .

❷ The most important recent **development** in technology is

_____ .

❸ I couldn't go to the _____ , so my friend texted me

frequently to let me know about any **developments**.

❹ _____ is a useful online tool for following **developments**

in the lives of people I know.

Writing Practice

Collaborate **Work with your partner** to complete the sentences using the correct form of **development** and appropriate content.

➀ Our school should work on the _____ of a _____ program.

➁ When there is a recent _____ in someone's life such as a breakup, other

people usually find out about it from _____ .

Your Turn **Work independently** to complete the sentences using the correct form of **development** and appropriate content.

➀ The _____ of an interesting story or movie is usually marked by a

dramatic event such as _____ .

➁ One recent _____ in my life is that I _____ .

Be an Academic Author **Work independently** to write two sentences. In your first sentence, use **development** in the *singular form*. In your second sentence, use **development** in the *plural form*.

MEANING ➀ _____

_____

MEANING ➁ _____

_____

grammar tip

Count nouns name things that can be counted. Count nouns have two forms, singular and plural. To make most count nouns plural, add –s.

I like to follow news development**s** online.

He likes board games.

Write an Academic Paragraph **Complete** the paragraph using the correct form of **development** and original content.

From scripted dramas to sitcoms, a significant amount of _____ ➀

goes into a TV episode before it airs. Each episode starts with an idea that writers

_____ into a script. Then, editors make sure the script is not too ➁

short or too _____ for the time slot. Once the script is final, actors ➂

_____ their lines and consider the _____ of ➃ ➄

their characters. Meanwhile, dozens of people _____ behind the scenes ➅

to produce costumes, scenery, and sound effects. The _____ of just a ➆

few minutes of entertainment requires many people working together.

77

elaborate
verb

▶ **Say it:** e • **lab** • o • rate   **Write it:** _____

Meaning	Example
to give more details about something	The _____ officer wasn't sure what the missing _____ looked like, so he asked the owner to **elaborate.**
Synonyms: develop, expand	

Forms		Family
Present: I/You/We/They elaborate He/She/It elaborates		• **Noun:** elaboration • **Adjective:** elaborate • **Adverb:** elaborately
Past: elaborated		

Word Partners

- decline to _____   The actress **declined to elaborate** on her reasons for quitting the film.
- refuse to _____   My dad said I couldn't borrow the car on Saturday, but when I asked him why, he **refused to elaborate**.

Verbal Practice

Talk about It **Read** each sentence and **think** about how you would complete it.

Discuss your idea with your partner using the sentence frame.

Listen carefully to your partner's and classmates' ideas.

Write your favorite idea in the blank.

❶ My teacher asked me to **elaborate** on my description of the book I read because I didn't include enough _____ .

❷ If someone I didn't know well asked me for more information about myself, I would refuse to **elaborate** because _____ .

Writing Practice

Collaborate **Work with your partner** to complete the sentence using the correct form of **elaborate** and appropriate content.

If I had to _____ on why I like my neighborhood, I would say that I

enjoy _____ .

Your Turn **Work independently** to complete the sentence using the correct form of **elaborate** and appropriate content.

I really wanted to know why my friend _____ ,

but she declined to _____ .

Be an Academic Author **Work independently** to write two sentences. In your first sentence, use **elaborate** in the *simple past tense*. In your second sentence, use **elaborate** with the word partner *refuse to elaborate*.

❶ _____

_____

❷ _____

_____

> ## grammar tip
>
> **To make the simple past tense of regular verbs, add –*ed* or –*d*.**
>
> She elaborat**ed** on the points in her essay.
>
> I play**ed** tennis today.

Write an Academic Paragraph **Complete** the paragraph using the correct form of **elaborate** and original content.

Speaking in front of an audience can be _____ ❶ , especially for

people who are _____ ❷ . However, if you prepare well, you can give a

successful speech. First, you should brainstorm ideas and research your topic. If you are giving

a persuasive speech, develop your best arguments and gather _____ ❸

to back up your opinions. Next, take notes and organize them. Keep your notes short so you

can use them as a quick reference; you should _____ ❹ on your points

in the speech itself. Finally, rehearse your speech in front of a _____ ❺ .

Be prepared to answer follow-up questions from the _____ ❻ after your

speech—you may be asked to _____ ❼ on some of the points you made.

emphasis
noun

▶ *Say it:* **em** • pha • sis

Write it: _____

Academic Vocabulary Toolkit

Meaning	Example	
the special importance given to something	Our science teacher puts a lot of **emphasis** on _____ whenever we work with _____ in class.	
Synonym: significance		

Forms	Family
• *Singular:* emphasis	• *Verb:* emphasize
• *Plural:* emphases	• *Adjective:* emphatic

Word Partners	
• greater _____	Our Spanish teacher puts **greater emphasis** on developing our conversation skills than doing vocabulary drills.
• place _____ on something	Our school **places emphasis on** students becoming global citizens.
• put an _____ on something	My parents **put an emphasis on** schoolwork over everything else.

Verbal Practice

Talk about It   **Read** each sentence and **think** about how you would complete it.

Discuss your idea with your partner using the sentence frame.

Listen carefully to your partner's and classmates' ideas.

Write your favorite idea in the blank.

❶ Of all my hobbies, I put the most **emphasis** on _____ because it's my favorite.

❷ In an English class, the teacher usually places **emphasis** on reading _____ and writing _____ .

Writing Practice

Collaborate **Work with your partner** to complete the sentence using the correct form of **emphasis** and appropriate content.

Our school should put less _____ on grades and greater _____

on _____ .

Your Turn **Work independently** to complete the sentence using the correct form of **emphasis** and appropriate content.

When I am 40 years old, I think the main _____ in my life will be on

_____ .

Be an Academic Author **Work independently** to write two sentences. In your first sentence, use **emphasis** in the *singular form*. In your second sentence, use **emphasis** with the word partner *put an emphasis on*.

❶ _____

_____

❷ _____

_____

> **grammar tip**
>
> The plural form of *emphasis, emphases,* is rarely used in speaking or writing.

Write an Academic Paragraph **Complete** the paragraph using the correct form of **emphasis** and original content.

It can be _____ to balance your school life and your personal life.
❶

You can't put greater _____ on one part of your life over the other
❷

because both of them are _____ . However, with proper planning, you
❸

can make sure that you give enough _____ to both. Some students
❹

find it helpful to make detailed _____ that list all of their priorities in
❺

order of importance. Other students _____ schedules that help them
❻

keep track of the different activities in their life, such as _____ and
❼

doing homework. Whichever method you choose to manage the different parts of your life,

finding a balance will help you make time to enjoy them all.

emphasize
verb

Write it: _____

Meaning	Example
to give something special importance	When I study, I use a _____ to **emphasize** important information that I want to _____ later.
Synonyms: stress, highlight	
Antonym: de-emphasize	

Forms		Family
Present:		• *Noun:* emphasis
I/You/We/They	emphasize	
He/She/It	emphasizes	
Past:	emphasized	

Word Partners

• _____ (my/your/his/her/our/their) point	The speaker **emphasized her point** by showing pictures of the disaster.
• _____ the importance of something	Our gym teacher **emphasizes the importance of** stretching before we exercise.
• _____ the need for something	I think all the litter on our school grounds **emphasizes the need for** more trash cans.

Verbal Practice

Talk about It **Read** each sentence and **think** about how you would complete it.

Discuss your idea with your partner using the sentence frame.

Listen carefully to your partner's and classmates' ideas.

Write your favorite idea in the blank.

❶ Some women use makeup to **emphasize** their _____ .

❷ When people argue, they often **emphasize** a point by _____ .

Writing Practice

Collaborate | **Work with your partner** to complete the sentence using the correct form of **emphasize** and appropriate content.

My doctor always _____ the importance of _____ .

Your Turn | **Work independently** to complete the sentence using the correct form of **emphasize** and appropriate content.

If I could change anything in my neighborhood, I would _____ the need for

more _____ .

Be an Academic Author | **Work independently** to write two sentences. In your first sentence, use **emphasize** in the *simple present tense* with a person's name. In your second sentence, use **emphasize** with the modal verb *would* and include a word partner.

❶ _____

_____

❷ _____

_____

> ## grammar tip
>
> In the simple present tense, the third-person singular (*he/she/it*) form takes an *–s* or *–es* ending.
>
> Mr. Tom emphasize**s** the importance of checking our work.
>
> She go**es** to the library after school.

Write an Academic Paragraph | **Complete** the paragraph using the correct form of **emphasize** and original content.

The Wodaabe, a nomadic tribe in Niger and Nigeria, are famous for their unique

_____ about beauty. Every year, men and women gather for Gerewol,
    ❶

a courtship festival during which men _____ elaborate makeup,
    ❷

jewelry, and clothing in order to attract a wife. In the Wodaabe culture, men are considered

_____ if they have white eyes and teeth and a long neck and
    ❸

nose. As a result, men will wear bright makeup on their faces and roll their eyes in order to

_____ the whiteness of their eyes and teeth. They may also paint a line
    ❹

down their nose to _____ its length. Throughout the festival, men flash
    ❺

their teeth and dance in an attempt to _____ their grace and charm,
    ❻

each hoping a woman will select him as her _____ .
    ❼

essential
adjective

▶ **Say it:** es • **sen** • tial   **Write it:** _____

Academic Vocabulary Toolkit

Meaning	Example	
necessary or very important	A _____ and a sleeping bag are **essential** items for _____ .	
Antonym: nonessential		

Family

- **Noun:** essence
- **Adverb:** essentially

Word Partners

• absolutely _____	When you ride in a car, it is **absolutely essential** that you wear a seatbelt.
• _____ part of	Emotions are an **essential part of** being human.
• play an _____ role	Citizen protests **played an essential role** in the downfall of the Tunisian and Egyptian governments in 2011.

Verbal Practice

Talk about It **Read** each sentence and **think** about how you would complete it.

Discuss your idea with your partner using the sentence frame.

Listen carefully to your partner's and classmates' ideas.

Write your favorite idea in the blank.

❶ If you're going on a long bus trip, it's absolutely **essential** to bring

_____ .

❷ _____ is an **essential** ingredient in cake.

Writing Practice

Collaborate **Work with your partner** to complete the sentence using **essential** and appropriate content.

_____ every day plays an _____ role in

doing well in school.

Your Turn **Work independently** to complete the sentence using **essential** and appropriate content.

Clothes like _____ and accessories like _____

are _____ parts of my personal style.

Be an Academic Author **Work independently** to write two sentences. In your first sentence, use **essential** with the word partner *essential part of*. In your second sentence, use **essential** with a *plural noun*.

❶ _____

_____

❷ _____

_____

> **grammar tip**
>
> Adjectives do not have plural forms. Do not add an *–s* to adjectives when they describe plural nouns.
>
> <u>essential</u> elements
> <u>loud</u> dogs

Write an Academic Paragraph **Complete** the paragraph using **essential** and original content.

Eating nutritious food is important for anyone to stay _____ , but

❶

do you know which nutrients are _____ for growing teenagers?

❷

Carbohydrates and protein, which you can find in oatmeal, pasta, fish, and tofu, are important

for _____ strong bones, muscles, and organs. Another important

❸

nutrient is calcium, which fortifies your bones and _____ . Try eating

❹

kale and Greek yogurt to increase your calcium intake. Next, dietary fats regulate cell structures

and hormones, and nutrients like zinc and B-12, which are plentiful in asparagus and broccoli,

are _____ for maintaining a responsive immune system. Finally, iron

❺

_____ support growth spurts and muscle mass increases. You can get

❻

more iron by eating red meat, spinach, and lentils. If teens _____ these

❼

nutrients every day as part of a well-balanced diet, they are sure to grow into healthy adults.

evidence
noun

▶ *Say it:* **ev • i • dence**   *Write it:* _____

Meaning	Example
anything that proves something is true *Synonyms:* proof, support	_____ made more money than any other movie in history, which is **evidence** that it was a very _____ movie.

Family

- *Adjective:* evident
- *Adverb:* evidently

Word Partners

• _____ suggests	**Evidence suggests** that drinking coffee every day has many health benefits.
• gather _____	The police officers **gathered evidence** at the scene of the accident.
• present _____	The lawyer **presented evidence** to the jury that her client was not guilty.

Verbal Practice

Talk about It   **Read** each sentence and **think** about how you would complete it.

Discuss your idea with your partner using the sentence frame.

Listen carefully to your partner's and classmates' ideas.

Write your favorite idea in the blank.

❶ When you write a paper for class, you have to present **evidence** to support your

_____ .

❷ If I'm going to accuse someone of _____ , I need to find

evidence first.

Writing Practice

Collaborate **Work with your partner** to complete the sentence using **evidence** and appropriate content.

When police detectives try to solve crimes, they gather _____ such

as _____ or _____ .

Your Turn **Work independently** to complete the sentence using **evidence** and appropriate content.

If someone asked me to present _____ that I am good at _____ ,

I would show them _____ as proof.

Be an Academic Author **Work independently** to write two sentences. In your first sentence, use **evidence** with the word partner *gather evidence*. In your second sentence, use **evidence** with the word partner *present evidence*.

❶ _____

_____

❷ _____

_____

> ## grammar tip
>
> **Non-count nouns name things that can't be counted. Non-count nouns have only one form. Do not add an –s to a non-count noun.**
>
> They don't have enough **evidence** to arrest her.
>
> The **water** is frozen.

Write an Academic Paragraph **Complete** the paragraph using **evidence** and original content.

Whether you're debating an issue with a friend or writing a persuasive essay, there

are two types of _____ that you can use to support your
❶

_____ . The first kind of evidence is scientific evidence, which includes
❷

examples from research studies, _____ articles, and other data. This
❸

type of _____ is very compelling because it usually comes from expert
❹

professionals or organizations. The second type of _____ is personal
❺

experience, which involves describing something that you have _____
❻

and relating it to your argument. For example, if someone argues that most people are

_____ , you could describe a time when a stranger did something nice
❼

for you. If you use these two kinds of evidence to support your argument, others will find it

much more persuasive and compelling.

expert
noun

Say it: **ex** • pert   **Write it:** _____

Academic Vocabulary Toolkit

Meaning	Example
someone who has special skills or knowledge about a subject	Many wildlife **experts** believe that _____ bears could be extinct by _____ .

Forms	Family
• *Singular:* expert • *Plural:* experts	• *Noun:* expertise • *Adjective:* expert • *Adverb:* expertly

Word Partners

• consult an _____	If you have a problem with your car, you should **consult an expert**.
• _____ in the field of	A pediatrician is an **expert in the field of** children's medicine.
• leading _____	My uncle is a **leading expert** in urban pollution and is often invited to appear on talk shows about the subject.

Verbal Practice

Talk about It   **Read** each sentence and **think** about how you would complete it.

Discuss your idea with your partner using the sentence frame.

Listen carefully to your partner's and classmates' ideas.

Write your favorite idea in the blank.

❶ If you break something valuable, such as your _____ , it's a good idea to consult an **expert** about repairing it.

❷ You don't have to be a computer **expert** to know that you should always

_____ .

88

Writing Practice

Collaborate **Work with your partner** to complete the sentence using the correct form of **expert** and appropriate content.

In our class, _____ and _____ are _____ on music.

Your Turn **Work independently** to complete the sentence using the correct form of **expert** and appropriate content.

One day I would like to become a leading _____ in the field of

_____ .

Be an Academic Author **Work independently** to write two sentences. In your first sentence, use **expert** in the *singular form* and include a word partner. In your second sentence, use **expert** in the *plural form*.

❶ _____

_____

❷ _____

_____

> ### grammar tip
>
> **Count nouns name things that can be counted. Count nouns have two forms, singular and plural. To make most count nouns plural, add –s.**
>
> Animal expert**s** agree that manatees are endangered.
>
> He likes board game**s**.

Write an Academic Paragraph **Complete** the paragraph using the correct form of **expert** and original content.

Detectives are _____ at solving crimes. In fiction, detectives
❶

such as _____ usually work alone or with a partner. They solve
❷

cases by searching for _____ and using their expertise to quickly
❸

catch _____ . However, in real life, detectives may investigate
❹

a case for years and work with many other _____ in the search
❺

for answers. For example, when a case goes to trial, detectives often rely on forensics

_____ to lend their expertise about evidence such as fingerprints
❻

or _____ . While detectives are experts at solving crimes, they still
❼

have to _____ experts in other fields in order to fully investigate all
❽

evidence and charge someone with a crime.

expertise
noun

▶ **Say it:** ex • per • **tise**　　　　*Write it:* _____

Meaning	Example
special skills or knowledge about a subject	A veterinarian's area of **expertise** is _____ .

Family

- *Noun:* expert
- *Adjective:* expert
- *Adverb:* expertly

Word Partners

• area of _____	Basketball is LeBron James's **area of expertise**.
• gain _____	I am hoping to **gain expertise** in computers so I can become a software programmer.
• share (my/your/his/her/our/their) _____	Next week a zoologist is going to visit our biology class and **share her expertise** on endangered animals.

Verbal Practice

Talk about It　**Read** each sentence and **think** about how you would complete it.

Discuss your idea with your partner using the sentence frame.

Listen carefully to your partner's and classmates' ideas.

Write your favorite idea in the blank.

❶ If you want to be a doctor, you need to gain **expertise** in _____ .

❷ My teacher knows a lot, but I don't think _____ is within _____ area of **expertise**.

Writing Practice

Collaborate **Work with your partner** to complete the sentence using **expertise** and appropriate content.

When I have problems with _____ , I usually ask someone I trust, like

my _____ , to lend his or her _____ .

Your Turn **Work independently** to complete the sentence using **expertise** and appropriate content.

_____ is definitely within my area of _____ .

Be an Academic Author **Work independently** to write two sentences. In your first sentence, use **expertise** with the word partner *area of expertise*. In your second sentence, use **expertise** with the word partner *gain expertise*.

❶ _____

_____

❷ _____

_____

grammar tip

Non-count nouns name things that can't be counted. Non-count nouns have only one form. Do not add an *–s* to a non-count noun.

Art is my area of **expertise**.

The **water** is frozen.

Write an Academic Paragraph **Complete** the paragraph using **expertise** and original content.

The Internet is a valuable resource for finding information. When you research information

online, you can benefit from the _____ of people from all over the

　　　　　　　　　　　　　　　　❶

world. However, how can you be sure that you are actually reading information provided

by _____ ? Anyone can _____ information

　　　❷　　　　　　　　　　　　　　　　　　❸

on the Internet and claim to be an expert without having to prove anything. One way to

_____ that you are getting expert information is to go to Web sites

　　　　❹

hosted by universities, libraries, and reputable educational organizations. These Web sites are

written and edited by experts who provide credible information from research and studies

and cite their _____ . If you need help _____

　　　　　　　　　❺　　　　　　　　　　　　　　　　　　　❻

reputable Web sites, librarians are a useful resource since finding information is their area of

_____ .

　　　❼

explain
verb

Academic Vocabulary Toolkit

Meaning	Example
to give details or reasons for something so that someone can understand it	My math _____ **explained** the _____ problem to me.

Forms

Present:	
I/You/We/They	explain
He/She/It	explains
Past:	explained

Family

- **Noun:** explanation
- **Adjective:** explanatory

Word Partners

• _____ how	Our computer science teacher **explained how** computers use binary codes to function.
• _____ why	The research team published a report **explaining why** the bee population is decreasing.
• help _____	Scientists believe that studying dolphins's brains may **help explain** how human intelligence works.

Verbal Practice

Talk about It   **Read** each sentence and **think** about how you would complete it.

Discuss your idea with your partner using the sentence frame.

Listen carefully to your partner's and classmates' ideas.

Write your favorite idea in the blank.

❶ Our teacher recently **explained** how to _____ .

❷ I know a lot about _____ , so I could **explain** it to a younger student.

Writing Practice

Collaborate **Work with your partner** to complete the sentence using the correct form of **explain** and appropriate content.

Most teenagers could easily _____ how to _____

if one of their older relatives didn't know how.

Your Turn **Work independently** to complete the sentence using the correct form of **explain** and appropriate content.

If I had to _____ why I enjoy playing _____ , I would say it is

because _____ .

Be an Academic Author **Work independently** to write two sentences. In your first sentence, use **explain** with the modal verb *could*. In your second sentence, use **explain** in the *simple past tense* and include a word partner.

❶ _____

_____

❷ _____

_____

> **grammar tip**
>
> Modal verbs are helping verbs that give additional meaning to the main verb. *Could* can be used to express future possibility.
>
> I **could** explain that to you later.
>
> She **could go** tomorrow.

Write an Academic Paragraph **Complete** the paragraph using the correct form of **explain** and original content.

Long ago, ancient cultures developed myths to _____
❶

natural phenomena like the rising and setting of the sun. For example, the Greeks

believed that the sun god Helios rode across the sky in a chariot every day, bringing the

_____ up or down with him. Similarly, ancient Egyptians believed
❷

that the sun god Ra _____ across the sky in a boat during the day.
❸

Another myth about the sun originates from the Navajo people of the southwestern United

States, who _____ that the god Tsohanoai carried the sun across the
❹

sky on his back during the day and hung it up inside his house at night. However, today we

use _____ instead of myths to _____ this
❺   ❻

phenomenon. We know that the sun rises and sets as the Earth _____
❼

on its axis.

93

explanation

noun

▶ **Say it:** ex • pla • **na** • tion   **Write it:** _____

<table>
<tr><th colspan="2">Meaning</th><th colspan="2">Example</th></tr>
</table>

Meaning	Example
a description or reason that you give to make something easier to understand	When Brian _____ the car home with a dented _____ , his parents demanded an **explanation**.

Academic Vocabulary Toolkit

Forms	Family
• *Singular:* explanation • *Plural:* explanations	• *Verb:* explain • *Adjective:* explanatory

Word Partners

• give an _____	Our coach demanded that Mark **give an explanation** for why he had missed so many practices.
• logical _____	One **logical explanation** for why some children are scared of the dark is that they have active imaginations.
• provide an _____	The video **provided an explanation** for why dolphins in the Amazon river have pink skin.

Verbal Practice

Talk about It   **Read** each sentence and **think** about how you would complete it.

Discuss your idea with your partner using the sentence frame.

Listen carefully to your partner's and classmates' ideas.

Write your favorite idea in the blank.

❶ A logical **explanation** for why some students fall asleep in class is that they

_____ .

❷ My friend asked me for an **explanation** after I

_____ .

Writing Practice

Collaborate **Work with your partner** to complete the sentence using the correct form of **explanation** and appropriate content.

If your stomach feels upset, two logical _____ might be that you

_____ or _____ .

Your Turn **Work independently** to complete the sentence using the correct form of **explanation** and appropriate content.

If you are late for _____ , you should give a valid _____ such as

" _____ ."

Be an Academic Author **Work independently** to write two sentences. In your first sentence, use **explanation** in the *singular form*. In your second sentence, use **explanation** in the *plural form* and include a word partner.

❶ _____

_____

❷ _____

_____

> ### grammar tip
>
> Count nouns name things that can be counted. Count nouns have two forms, singular and plural. To make most count nouns plural, add –s.
>
> There are many possible explanation**s**.
>
> He likes board game**s**.

Write an Academic Paragraph **Complete** the paragraph using the correct form of **explanation** and original content.

About 65 million _____ ago, a large number of animal and
⓵

plant species—including all the dinosaurs—suddenly went extinct. No one knows exactly

why this happened, but _____ have offered several possible
⓶

_____ . The most widely accepted _____ is that
⓷ ⓸

Earth was hit by one or more giant asteroids. As evidence of this, several large craters dating to

65 million years ago have been _____ . One is the Chicxulub crater in
⓹

Mexico, which is about 111 miles wide and one mile deep and would have caused catastrophic

damage upon impact. Whatever the full _____ for the extinction of
⓺

the dinosaurs, those events made way for a new era of _____ on
⓻

Earth: humans.

factor
noun

Write it: _____

Academic Vocabulary Toolkit

Meaning	Example
something that affects a situation	Not wearing protective _____ is often a **factor**
Synonyms: cause, reason	in _____ injuries.

Forms	Family
• *Singular:* factor • *Plural:* factors	• *Verb:* factor

Word Partners

• contributing _____	Texting while driving is a **contributing factor** in many car accidents.
• key _____	The thunderstorm was a **key factor** in our decision to cancel the picnic.
• significant _____	Price will be a **significant factor** in what I decide to get my best friend for his birthday.

Verbal Practice

Talk about It **Read** each sentence and **think** about how you would complete it.

Discuss your idea with your partner using the sentence frame.

Listen carefully to your partner's and classmates' ideas.

Write your favorite idea in the blank.

❶ One **factor** that can contribute to a bad grade on a test is

_____ .

❷ _____ and _____ are two **factors**

that your teacher considers when he or she calculates your final grade.

Writing Practice

Collaborate **Work with your partner** to complete the sentence using the correct form of **factor** and appropriate content.

_____ is often a contributing _____ to poor health.

Your Turn **Work independently** to complete the sentence using the correct form of **factor** and appropriate content.

Time is a key _____ in whether or not I can participate in

_____ during the school year.

Be an Academic Author **Work independently** to write two sentences. In your first sentence, use **factor** in the *singular form* and include a word partner. In your second sentence, use **factor** in the *plural form*.

❶ _____

_____

❷ _____

_____

> **grammar tip**
>
> **Count nouns name things that can be counted. Count nouns have two forms, singular and plural. To make most count nouns plural, add –s.**
>
> There were many contributing factor**s** to the team's loss.
>
> He likes board games.

Write an Academic Paragraph **Complete** the paragraph using the correct form of **factor** and original content.

Depression is a serious illness that _____ millions of teenagers

❶

and adults in the United States. There are a number of genetic and environmental

_____ that can contribute to depression. First, if your mother or father

❷

had depression, there is an increased _____ that you will develop it

❸

also. Second, if you suffer from anxiety, you are also more likely to _____

❹

depression. Third, a wide variety of environmental _____

❺

can trigger episodes of depression. These include the loss of a loved one, such as a

_____ , experiencing emotional or physical trauma, and suffering

❻

abuse. Although none of these _____ guarantees that you will become

❼

depressed, it is important to be aware of the possibility and contact a mental health professional

if you suspect that you or someone you know is experiencing depression.

identify
verb

Academic Vocabulary Toolkit

Meaning	Example
to recognize or say what something is	The witness **identified** the _____ who had stolen
Synonym: distinguish	his _____ .

Forms		Family
Present:		• **Noun:** identification
I/You/We/They	identify	• **Adjective:** identifiable
He/She/It	identifies	• **Adverb:** identifiably
Past:	identified	

Word Partners

• difficult to _____	Sometimes it is **difficult to identify** the cause of an illness without performing multiple tests on a patient.
• _____ a factor	The researchers **identified factors** that may endanger the quality of the city's drinking water.
• _____ a/the problem	My mother **identified the problem** with our air conditioner and fixed it.

Verbal Practice

Talk about It **Read** each sentence and **think** about how you would complete it.

Discuss your idea with your partner using the sentence frame.

Listen carefully to your partner's and classmates' ideas.

Write your favorite idea in the blank.

❶ When I look at the sky at night, I can **identify** _____ .

❷ In science class, we **identified** the anatomy of a _____ .

Writing Practice

Collaborate **Work with your partner** to complete the sentence using the correct form of **identify** and appropriate content.

I can _____ most _____ within ten seconds of

seeing them.

Your Turn **Work independently** to complete the sentence using the correct form of **identify** and appropriate content.

I _____ the problem with my _____ and repaired it.

Be an **Work independently** to write two sentences. In your first sentence, use **identify** with the modal verb
Academic *can*. In your second sentence, use **identify** in the *simple past tense*.
Author

❶ _____

_____

❷ _____

_____

> ## grammar tip
>
> **Modal verbs are helping verbs that give additional meaning to the main verb.** *Can* **often expresses ability.**
>
> Sarah <u>**can**</u> **identify** what kind of flower that is.
>
> I <u>**can**</u> **fix** bicycles.

Write an **Complete** the paragraph using the correct form of **identify** and original
Academic content.
Paragraph

Some people have a _____ known as perfect pitch—the ability to
                                    ❶

_____ any musical note that is played just by listening. People with
          ❷

perfect pitch can also _____ the pitches of ordinary noises such as car
                              ❸

horns and bird calls. Others can even produce specific pitches on their own without any external

help. For example, if you ask them to sing the note _____ , they can
                                                          ❹

do it without hearing the note first. Understandably, perfect pitch is a skill often possessed by

musicians and _____ . However, scientists believe that people aren't
                    ❺

born with perfect pitch; instead, these people probably _____ to
                                                                  ❻

identify pitches after being exposed to music at an early _____ .
                                                                ❼

identity
noun

Say it: i • **den** • ti • ty   Write it: _____

Meanings	Examples
1. a person's name	1. Teenage students can use a _____ ID or a driver's license to _____ their **identity**.
2. the qualities or characteristics of a person or group	2. People in the _____ have a wide _____ of cultural **identities**.

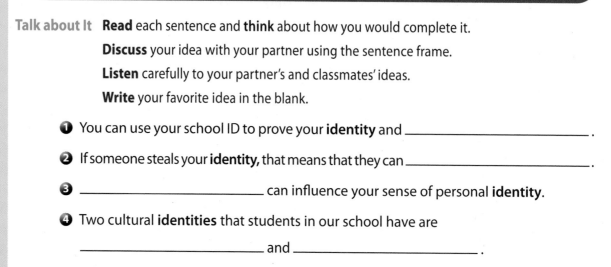

Forms	Family
• *Singular:* identity • *Plural:* identities	• *Verb:* identify • *Adjective:* identifiable • *Adverb:* identifiably

Word Partners

• cultural _____	Ana's **cultural identity** is Polish and American because her parents are from Poland, but she grew up in the United States.
• personal _____	My **personal identity** is informed by my love of Japanese culture.
• sense of _____	Your **sense of identity** can revolve around many factors: where you are from, your religion, your gender, and more.

Academic Vocabulary Toolkit

Verbal Practice

Talk about It **Read** each sentence and **think** about how you would complete it.

Discuss your idea with your partner using the sentence frame.

Listen carefully to your partner's and classmates' ideas.

Write your favorite idea in the blank.

❶ You can use your school ID to prove your **identity** and _____ .

❷ If someone steals your **identity,** that means that they can _____ .

❸ _____ can influence your sense of personal **identity**.

❹ Two cultural **identities** that students in our school have are

_____ and _____ .

Writing Practice

Collaborate   **Work with your partner** to complete the sentence using the correct form of **identity** and appropriate content.

One way that people express their personal _____ is by wearing

_____ .

Your Turn   **Work independently** to complete the sentence using the correct form of **identity** and appropriate content.

I think that my cultural background _____ formed a large part of my

_____ because _____ .

Be an Academic Author   **Work independently** to write two sentences. In your first sentence, use **identity** in the *singular form*. In your second sentence, use **identity** in the *plural form* and include a word partner.

❶ _____

_____

❷ _____

_____

> **grammar tip**
>
> To form the plural of a noun that ends in a consonant + *y*, change the *y* to *i* and add –*es*.
>
> identity—identit**ies**
>
> puppy—pupp**ies**

Write an Academic Paragraph   **Complete** the paragraph using the correct form of **identity** and original content.

Singapore is a small country in southeast Asia. Although only five million people

live there, Singapore has a wide range of cultural _____ due
❶

to its close proximity to other Asian nations. Most Singaporeans are of Chinese, Indian,

or Malay _____ , and as a result, Singapore has four official
❷

_____ : English, Chinese, Malay, and Tamil. Singapore's mixture of
❸

cultural _____ is also reflected in the culinary and religious preferences
❹

of its population. For example, a popular _____ of food called
❺

Peranakan is a hybrid of Chinese and Malay cuisine. Singaporeans also practice a wide range

of _____ , including Buddhism, Christianity, Islam, and Taoism, which
❻

reflects Eastern and Western influences on the population. Singapore may be a tiny nation, but

its residents have a fascinating array of cultural _____ .
❼

impact
noun

▶ **Say it:** **im** • pact   **Write it:** _____

Meanings	Examples
1. the force with which one object hits another	**1.** The _____ of the meteor's **impact** was so great that it left an enormous crater in the _____ .
2. a strong effect **Synonyms:** influence, impression	**2.** Teachers can have a _____ **impact** on their students' lives.

Forms	Family
• **Singular:** impact • **Plural:** impacts	• **Verb:** impact

Word Partners	
• have an _____	My gymnastics coach has **had an impact** on my life since I was young.
• make an _____	The new recycling law will **make an impact** on the city's litter problem.
• positive/negative _____	The recent oil spill had a **negative impact** on the fishing industry.

Verbal Practice

Talk about It   **Read** each sentence and **think** about how you would complete it.

Discuss your idea with your partner using the sentence frame.

Listen carefully to your partner's and classmates' ideas.

Write your favorite idea in the blank.

❶ The **impact** from two cars colliding can cause injuries such as

_____ .

❷ If a _____ hit the earth, the **impact** could destroy many homes.

❸ Natural disasters such as _____ can have a major **impact** on a region for years to come.

❹ Inventions like _____ have had positive **impacts** on the environment.

Writing Practice

Collaborate **Work with your partner** to complete the sentence using the correct form of **impact** and appropriate content.

Activities like _____ and _____ can have negative

_____ on your health.

Your Turn **Work independently** to complete the sentence using the correct form of **impact** and appropriate content.

Someone who has had an important _____ on my life is my _____

because _____ .

Be an Academic Author **Work independently** to write two sentences using Meaning 2 of **impact**. In your first sentence, use **impact** in the *singular form* and include a word partner. In your second sentence, use **impact** in the *plural form*.

❶ _____

_____

❷ _____

_____

Write an Academic Paragraph **Complete** the paragraph using the correct form of **impact** and original content.

Documentaries are movies that film real-life situations, usually with

the _____ of educating people about a subject. Many documentaries
      ❶

have a wide _____ on the public because they focus on important or
      ❷

controversial issues, such as the environmental impacts of _____ .
      ❸

One influential documentary was the 2005 film *500 Years Later,* which explored the

_____ of historical and contemporary issues affecting people of
      ❹

African descent. This film had a significant _____ because of its
      ❺

unique storytelling style and historical documentation of slavery. Documentaries like this

have the _____ to shed light on noteworthy subjects and can even
      ❻

_____ legislation.
      ❼

include
verb

▶ **Say it:** in • **clude**   **Write it:** _____

Academic Vocabulary Toolkit

Meaning	Example	
to make a part of something *Antonym:* exclude	I try to **include** all of my _____ whenever I organize an event.	☑ Mark Hogan ☑ Jason Pressler ☑ Maricruz Alvarez ❑ Robert Ilukowicz ❑ Francine Pellegrino ❑ Alfred Gonzalez

Forms		Family
Present: I/You/We/They include He/She/It includes *Past:* included		• *Noun:* inclusion • *Adjective:* inclusive • *Preposition:* including

Word Partners

• _____ the following: A basic first-aid kit should **include the following**: bandages, antibacterial ointment, and gauze pads.

Verbal Practice

Talk about It **Read** each sentence and **think** about how you would complete it.

Discuss your idea with your partner using the sentence frame.

Listen carefully to your partner's and classmates' ideas.

Write your favorite idea in the blank.

❶ I **included** _____ as part of my lunch today.

❷ One way to stay healthy is to **include** _____ in your daily routine.

Writing Practice

Collaborate

Work with a partner to complete the sentence using the correct form of **include** and appropriate content.

If I went hiking in the jungle, two things I would _____ in my backpack would

be _____ and _____ .

Your Turn

Work independently to complete the sentence using the correct form of **include** and appropriate content.

A good cell phone plan should _____ the following: unlimited

_____ and inexpensive _____ .

Be an Academic Author

Work independently to write two sentences. In your first sentence, use **include** in the *simple past tense*. In your second sentence, use **include** with the modal verb *should*.

❶ _____

_____

❷ _____

_____

> ### grammar tip
>
> Modal verbs are helping verbs that give additional meaning to the main verb. *Should* can be used to express advice.
>
> You **should** **include** some pictures in your report.
>
> She **should** **be** more careful.

Write an Academic Paragraph

Complete the paragraph using the correct form of **include** and original content.

Every family should have a disaster preparedness kit to help them plan for

_____ ❶ . This kit should _____ ❷ a list

of essential items to pack in case you and your family suddenly have to leave your

_____ ❸ . The most important items to _____ ❹

on this list are those that you need on a daily basis, such as medications. The next group

of items should _____ ❺ those that you need for identification

purposes, such as driver's licenses and _____ ❻ . Finally, your list could

_____ ❼ one or two irreplaceable mementos such as family photo

albums or _____ ❽ . Preparing this list in advance will enable your family

to evacuate quickly without leaving important items behind.

including
preposition

Academic Vocabulary Toolkit

Meaning	Example	
used to introduce examples that are part of a group	Tiffany plays many _____ , **including** basketball, softball, and _____ .	
Antonym: excluding		

Family

- *Noun:* inclusion
- *Verb:* include
- *Adjective:* inclusive

Word Partners

• _____ the following:	Students at our school speak several languages, **including the following**: Spanish, Creole, Vietnamese, and Farsi.

Verbal Practice

Talk about It **Read** each sentence and **think** about how you would complete it.

Discuss your idea with your partner using the sentence frame.

Listen carefully to your partner's and classmates' ideas.

Write your favorite idea in the blank.

1. There are many extracurricular sports and clubs at our school, **including** _____ and _____ .

2. Students should eat a breakfast with healthy food choices, **including** _____ .

Writing Practice

Collaborate   **Work with your partner** to complete the sentence using **including** and appropriate content.

Every year at school there are several _____ that students must take,

_____ English, math, and _____ .

Your Turn   **Work independently** to complete the sentence using **including** and appropriate content.

_____ offers many delicious flavors of ice cream, _____ the

following: _____ and _____ .

Be an Academic Author   **Work independently** to write two sentences. In your first sentence, use **including** with *two nouns*. In your second sentence, use **including** with the word partner *including the following* and *three nouns*.

❶ _____

_____

❷ _____

_____

> ## grammar tip
>
> **When writing a list, do not use a colon after *including*. Instead, use a colon after *including the following*.**
>
> I like many board games, **including** chess and go.
>
> You'll need a few items, **including the following:** pencils, paper, and glue.

Write an Academic Paragraph   **Complete** the paragraph using **including** and original content.

Mexico has some of the most diverse weather in the world,

_____ tropical and temperate zones and
    ❶

hurricanes. In the north, there are dry climates that _____ very little
                               ❷

rain, as well as tropical lowlands that can average nearly 80 inches of rainfall a year. In the

temperate zones to the south, _____ are much cooler, so many large
                              ❸

cities are located in these areas. In the southernmost _____ of Mexico,
                                 ❹

temperatures are steady year round, but both coasts _____ hurricanes.
                               ❺

In 2005, Hurricane Wilma _____ Mexico and caused significant
                        ❻

destruction, _____ the deaths of eight people. Nevertheless, Mexico
                ❼

remains a beautiful country that requires a little planning before you visit.

indicate
verb

▶ **Say it:** in • di • cate   **Write it:** _____

Academic Vocabulary Toolkit

Meanings	Examples
1. to show where or what something is *Synonyms:* gesture, signal	**1.** The woman **indicated** where the _____ was located by pointing down the _____ .
2. to show that something is probably true *Synonym:* demonstrate	**2.** Studies **indicate** that students who don't eat _____ are more likely to be _____ in the afternoon.

Forms		Family
Present: I/You/We/They indicate He/She/It indicates *Past:* indicated		• *Noun:* indication, indicator • *Adjective:* indicative

Word Partners

• research _____ s	**Research indicates** that girls have better fine motor skills than boys.
• studies _____	**Studies indicate** that exercising three times a week can help you lose weight.

Verbal Practice

Talk about It   **Read** each sentence and **think** about how you would complete it.

         Discuss your idea with your partner using the sentence frame.

         Listen carefully to your partner's and classmates' ideas.

         Write your favorite idea in the blank.

❶ Dogs often **indicate** that they want to go for a walk by _____ .

❷ In the cafeteria, your friends might **indicate** that they have a seat for you by _____ .

❸ Research **indicates** that texting while driving _____ .

❹ The survey results **indicated** that approximately _____ students at this school were involved in extracurricular activities last year.

Writing Practice

Collaborate **Work with your partner** to complete the sentence using the correct form of **indicate** and appropriate content.

The growing trend of obesity in America _____ that people need

to _____ .

Your Turn **Work independently** to complete the sentence using the correct form of **indicate** and appropriate content.

My last report card _____ that I am a _____ student who

did well in _____ .

Be an Academic Author **Work independently** to write two sentences using Meaning 2 of **indicate**. In your first sentence, use **indicate** in the *simple past tense*. In your second sentence, use **indicate** in the *simple present tense*.

❶ _____

_____

❷ _____

_____

> **grammar tip**
>
> **To make the simple past tense of regular verbs, add −ed or −d.**
>
> My grades indicat**ed** that I needed to study more.
>
> We play**ed** tennis today.

Write an Academic Paragraph **Complete** the paragraph using the correct form of **indicate** and original content.

Numerous studies have _____ the positive effects of exercise on
                                       ❶

physical health. However, new research _____ that exercise may
                                                    ❷

improve people's cognitive abilities as well. Researchers recently studied a group of overweight

students. First, they gave the _____ an intelligence test. Then, they
                                          ❸

_____ the students into two groups. The first group walked for 20 to
            ❹

40 minutes every day, while the other group didn't _____ at all. At
                                                                ❺

the end of the study, students took the intelligence test again. The scores of students who had

exercised increased, but students in the second group saw no _____ .
                                                                          ❻

These results _____ that exercise can improve both your physical and
                        ❼

cognitive health.

indication
noun

Say it: in • di • **ca** • tion **Write it:** _____

Meaning	Example
a sign of something	Gray clouds and _____ are **indications** that it is going to _____ .

Forms

- *Singular:* indication
- *Plural:* indications

Family

- *Noun:* indicator
- *Verb:* indicate
- *Adjective:* indicative

Word Partners

• clear _____	Test scores alone do not provide a **clear indication** of a student's academic ability.
• give an _____	The blood test will **give an indication** of whether or not you need to take iron supplements.
• no _____	Despite the predicted snowstorm, there is **no indication** that the principal is going to cancel school tomorrow.

Verbal Practice

Talk about It **Read** each sentence and **think** about how you would complete it.

Discuss your idea with your partner using the sentence frame.

Listen carefully to your partner's and classmates' ideas.

Write your favorite idea in the blank.

❶ A cough can be an **indication** that someone has

_____ .

❷ Two **indications** that someone is a good student are _____

and _____ .

Writing Practice

Collaborate   **Work with your partner** to complete the sentence using the correct form of **indication** and appropriate content.

Unfortunately, if your boyfriend or girlfriend _____ ,

that may be an _____ that he or she wants to break up with you.

Your Turn   **Work independently** to complete the sentence using the correct form of **indication** and appropriate content.

There are no _____ that mythical creatures such as _____

actually exist.

Be an   **Work independently** to write two sentences. In your first sentence, use **indication** in the *plural form*.
Academic   In your second sentence, use **indication** in the *singular form*.
Author

❶ _____

_____

❷ _____

_____

> **grammar tip**
>
> **Count nouns name things that can be counted. Count nouns have two forms, singular and plural. To make most count nouns plural, add –s.**
>
> There are no indications that aliens exist.
>
> He likes board games.

Write an   **Complete** the paragraph using the correct form of **indication** and original
Academic   content.
Paragraph

Children's everyday interests are sometimes _____ of the careers

❶

that they will have when they become _____ . A small number of

❷

children know from a very early age what they want to be when they grow up—such as an

astronaut, a veterinarian, or a _____—but a larger number of people

❸

pursue careers based on activities they enjoyed doing when they were young. For example,

someone who likes to paint or _____ might become an interior

❹

designer or an art teacher. Another person who enjoys building models may become an

architect or _____ . Childhood interests don't determine a person's

❺

future career, but they can _____ possible occupations that a person

❻

might enjoy as an adult.

introduce
verb

▶ **Say it:** in • tro • **duce**   **Write it:** _____

Meanings	Examples	
1. to meet a person and share names for the first time	1. Alex **introduced** himself to me at the _____ .	
2. to present something to someone for the first time **Synonym:** show	2. _____ companies **introduced** the first personal _____ in the 1970s.	

Forms		Family
Present: I/You/We/They introduce He/She/It introduces **Past:** introduced		• **Noun:** introduction • **Adjective:** introductory

Word Partners	
• _____ a change	The principal will **introduce changes** to the class and lunch schedules next month.

Verbal Practice

Talk about It   **Read** each sentence and **think** about how you would complete it.

Discuss your idea with your partner using the sentence frame.

Listen carefully to your partner's and classmates' ideas.

Write your favorite idea in the blank.

❶ If I met the singer _____ , I would feel too nervous to **introduce** myself.

❷ Two friends I **introduced** to each other were _____ and _____ .

❸ One activity that our school doesn't have but should **introduce** is _____ .

❹ Our English teacher recently **introduced** us to the book _____ .

Writing Practice

Collaborate   **Work with your partner** to complete the sentence using the correct form of **introduce** and appropriate content.

One class our school should _____ is _____

because _____ .

Your Turn   **Work independently** to complete the sentence using the correct form of **introduce** and appropriate content.

Every year, makers of snack foods _____ new products such as

_____ and _____ .

Be an Academic Author   **Work independently** to write two sentences using Meaning 2 of **introduce**. In your first sentence, use **introduce** with the modal verb *should*. In your second sentence, use **introduce** in the *simple past tense*.

❶ _____

_____

❷ _____

_____

> ## grammar tip
>
> **Modal verbs are helping verbs that give additional meaning to the main verb.** *Should* **can be used to express advice.**
>
> Our art teacher **should introduce** watercolors.
>
> They **should stop** talking.

Write an Academic Paragraph   **Complete** the paragraph using the correct form of **introduce** and original content.

Every fall, there are two major holiday celebrations in the United States: Halloween and

Thanksgiving. The traditions associated with these _____ were first
                                                     ❶

introduced many years ago. On Halloween, many children _____
              ❷

costumes and ask their neighbors for _____ . Historians believe
              ❸

that British and Irish immigrants _____ this tradition, called trick-
              ❹

or-treating, sometime in the early 1900s. On Thanksgiving, families typically eat a delicious

_____ of roast turkey. When the Pilgrims and the Wampanoag ate a
              ❺

large meal together at Plymouth in 1621, they _____ this tradition.
              ❻

Although these traditions were introduced centuries ago, they are still appreciated by many

_____ today.
  ❼

113

introduction

noun

Say it: in • tro • **duc** • tion   *Write it:* _____

Meanings	Examples
1. the act of meeting a person and sharing names for the first time	**1.** "Nice to _____ you!" is something a person often says _____ an **introduction** to someone else.
2. the first part of a book, paper, or speech that tells you what the topic is going to be *Synonym:* beginning	**2.** The U.S. _____ has a famous **introduction**.

Academic Vocabulary Toolkit

Forms	Family
• *Singular:* introduction • *Plural:* introductions	• *Verb:* introduce • *Adjective:* introductory

Word Partners	
• brief _____	I quickly skimmed the book's **brief introduction** before beginning the first chapter.

Verbal Practice

Talk about It   **Read** each sentence and **think** about how you would complete it.

Discuss your idea with your partner using the sentence frame.

Listen carefully to your partner's and classmates' ideas.

Write your favorite idea in the blank.

❶ People should _____ during an **introduction**.

❷ _____ needs no **introduction**—she's so popular that everyone knows who she is.

❸ The **introduction** of a textbook usually has information about _____ .

❹ The speaker had to wait for the _____ to stop before she could begin the **introduction** of her speech.

114

Writing Practice

Collaborate — **Work with your partner** to complete the sentence using the correct form of **introduction** and appropriate content.

The purpose of the _____ in an essay is to tell the reader

_____ .

Your Turn — **Work independently** to complete the sentence using the correct form of **introduction** and appropriate content.

I _____ read the _____ of my textbooks because

_____ .

Be an Academic Author — **Work independently** to write two sentences using Meaning 2 of **introduction**. In your first sentence, use **introduction** in the *singular form*. In your second sentence, use **introduction** in the *plural form*.

❶ _____

_____

❷ _____

_____

grammar tip

Count nouns name things that can be counted. Count nouns have two forms, singular and plural. To make most count nouns plural, add –s.

We had to rewrite our essay introductions.

He likes board games.

Write an Academic Paragraph — **Complete** the paragraph using the correct form of **introduction** and original content.

Whether you're writing a research paper or a _____ for class, it's
❶

important to begin your work with a strong _____ . In a shorter written
❷

piece, such as a paragraph, the introduction is usually your _____
❸

sentence. It's important for short _____ to be as concise and
❹

direct as possible. In contrast, _____ for essays and papers
❺

are much longer, usually one or two paragraphs. Longer introductions allow you to

_____ your topic with greater detail. No matter what you write,
❻

an excellent _____ helps your readers _____
❼   ❽

your argument and makes them want to keep reading.

issue
noun

▶ *Say it:* **is** • sue   *Write it:* _____

Meanings	Examples
1. a topic or problem that people talk about *Synonym:* subject	**1.** Homelessness is a _____ **issue** that impacts millions of _____ in the United States.
2. a specific edition of a newspaper or magazine	**2.** The _____ **issue** of this magazine has an interesting article about _____ .

Forms	Family
• *Singular:* issue • *Plural:* issues	• *Verb:* issue

Word Partners	
• discuss an _____	In our science class, we **discussed the issue** of global warming.
• important _____	Privacy is an **important issue** to consider if you use social networking Web sites.
• serious _____	Bullying is a **serious issue** that affects many young people.

Verbal Practice

Talk about It **Read** each sentence and **think** about how you would complete it.

Discuss your idea with your partner using the sentence frame.

Listen carefully to your partner's and classmates' ideas.

Write your favorite idea in the blank.

❶ One **issue** that I often discuss with my friends is _____ .

❷ _____ is one of the most important **issues** in the United States today.

❸ In the next **issue** of the school newspaper, I'd like to see an article about _____ .

❹ I enjoy reading each **issue** of the magazine _____ when it comes out.

Writing Practice

Collaborate   **Work with your partner** to complete the sentences using the correct form of **issue** and appropriate content.

❶ The most serious _____ affecting teenagers today is _____ .

❷ Today's _____ of the newspaper discussed _____ .

Your Turn   **Work independently** to complete the sentences using the correct form of **issue** and appropriate content.

❶ When people discuss environmental _____ , they often talk about

_____ .

❷ I would read a magazine _____ about _____ .

Be an Academic Author   **Work independently** to write two sentences. In your first sentence, use **issue** in the *plural form* and include a word partner. In your second sentence, use **issue** in the *singular form*.

MEANING ❶ _____

_____

MEANING ❷ _____

_____

> **grammar tip**
>
> Count nouns name things that can be counted. Count nouns have two forms, singular and plural. To make most count nouns plural, add –*s*.
>
> There are many issue**s** to consider.
>
> She has some question**s**.

Write an Academic Paragraph   **Complete** the paragraph using the correct form of **issue** and original content.

When people immigrate to the United States, there are a number of

_____ ❶ that they encounter. The biggest _____ ❷

is usually the language difference; it can be very _____ ❸ not to have the

ability to express yourself. Another _____ ❹ is the climate. For example,

when people move from tropical countries, such as _____ ❺ , to northern

states, the cold weather can be difficult to tolerate. A final _____ ❻ is

acclimating to cultural differences. Customs or behaviors that are appropriate in one place may

be considered _____ ❼ in another. While these issues may be obstacles

at first, most people _____ ❽ them and thrive in their new country.

justify
verb

Write it: _____

	Meaning	Example
Academic Vocabulary Toolkit	to give reasons why something is right or necessary	Most people can't **justify** spending _____ on a pair of _____ .

Forms		Family
Present:		• **Noun:** justification
I/You/We/They	justify	• **Adjective:** justifiable
He/She/It	justifies	• **Adverb:** justifiably
Past:	justified	

Word Partners

• _____ why	If you come to class after the bell rings, your teacher will probably ask you to **justify why** you are late.

Verbal Practice

Talk about It   **Read** each sentence and **think** about how you would complete it.

Discuss your idea with your partner using the sentence frame.

Listen carefully to your partner's and classmates' ideas.

Write your favorite idea in the blank.

❶ The principal **justified** expelling the student because _____ .

❷ I can **justify** spending $30 each month on a cell phone because

_____ .

Writing Practice

Collaborate **Work with your partner** to complete the sentence using the correct form of **justify** and appropriate content.

You can _____ lying to someone when _____ .

Your Turn **Work independently** to complete the sentence using the correct form of **justify** and appropriate content.

I _____ turning in my assignment late by telling my teacher that

_____ .

Be an **Work independently** to write two sentences. In your first sentence, use **justify** in the *simple past tense*.
Academic In your second sentence, use **justify** with the modal verb *can*.
Author

❶ _____

_____

❷ _____

_____

> **grammar tip**
>
> Modal verbs are helping verbs that give additional meaning to the main verb. *Can* often expresses ability.
>
> She **can justify** her decision.
>
> I **can fix** bicycles.

Write an **Complete** the paragraph using the correct form of **justify** and original content.
Academic
Paragraph Is war ever justified? Pacifists are people who argue that no country can ever

_____ initiating war because it can have _____
❶ ❷

impacts, including the death and displacement of innocent people. One powerful example

that many pacifists use to _____ their argument is the fact that
❸

several countries have access to nuclear weapons, which could _____
❹

millions of people and cause devastating environmental and health problems in a region

for years. However, other people argue that there are certain _____
❺

in which it is necessary to go to war. For instance, if a country is attacked, there is a clear

need for that country to _____ itself. Do you think there are any
❻

_____ in which war is justified?
❼

locate
verb

▶ **Say it:** **lo** • cate   **Write it:** _____

Meaning	Example
to find where something is	The teacher asked Michael to **locate** _____ on the map.

Forms	Family
Present: I/You/We/They locate He/She/It locates **Past:** located	• **Noun:** location

Word Partners
• difficult/easy to _____   It's **easy to locate** my house because it's the only one on my street that is painted purple.

Verbal Practice

Talk about It   **Read** each sentence and **think** about how you would complete it.

Discuss your idea with your partner using the sentence frame.

Listen carefully to your partner's and classmates' ideas.

Write your favorite idea in the blank.

❶ One way to **locate** where your classes are on the first day of school is to

_____ .

❷ Using a _____ , you can easily **locate** restaurants and stores

close to your house.

120

Writing Practice

Collaborate **Work with your partner** to complete the sentence using the correct form of **locate** and appropriate content.

Scientists use telescopes to _____ the exact position of _____ .

Your Turn **Work independently** to complete the sentence using the correct form of **locate** and appropriate content.

I _____ information for my last research paper using

_____ .

Be an Academic Author **Work independently** to write two sentences. In your first sentence, use **locate** in the *simple present tense*. In your second sentence, use **locate** in the *simple past tense*.

❶ _____

_____

❷ _____

_____

> ### grammar tip
> **To make the simple past tense of regular verbs, add –ed or –d.**
> I locat**ed** my notebook.
> We play**ed** tennis today.

Write an Academic Paragraph **Complete** the paragraph using the correct form of **locate** and original content.

The Internet has made it easier than ever to find information, but there are also negative

_____ to having certain information easily accessible. On one hand,
　　　　❶

the Internet is an unrivaled tool for finding _____ quickly. For example,
　　　　　　　　　　　　　　　　　　　　　　　　❷

if you need to _____ a doctor in your area or want the location of the
　　　　　　　　❸

nearest _____ , you can use your _____ to find
　　　　　❹　　　　　　　　　　　　　　　　　　　❺

this information online. On the other hand, the Internet has also made it significantly easier to

_____ private details, such as people's _____ .
　　　　❻　　　　　　　　　　　　　　　　　　　　　　　　❼

For instance, some people _____ that it is an invasion of privacy for
　　　　　　　　　　　　　　❽

photographs of their homes to be posted online. The Internet has many positive uses, but

users need to consider its drawbacks as well.

logical
adjective

▶ **Say it:** **log** • i • cal   **Write it:** _____

Meaning	Example
using careful reasoning or good sense	Adopting a _____ isn't a **logical** choice if you're _____ to them.
Synonyms: rational, sensible *Antonym:* illogical	

Family

- *Noun:* logic
- *Adverb:* logically

Word Partners

- _____ choice

  Since Veronica was Assistant Editor for the yearbook staff last year, making her Editor in Chief this year was a **logical choice**.

- _____ explanation

  Scientists have **logical explanations** for the causes of volcanic eruptions and earthquakes.

- _____ reason

  Two **logical reasons** for recycling are that it reduces garbage and allows us to reuse materials.

Verbal Practice

Talk about It   **Read** each sentence and **think** about how you would complete it.

Discuss your idea with your partner using the sentence frame.

Listen carefully to your partner's and classmates' ideas.

Write your favorite idea in the blank.

❶ One **logical** reason why parents give their children curfews is that

_____ .

❷ If you lose your wallet, a **logical** step in finding it is to

_____ .

Writing Practice

Collaborate **Work with your partner** to complete the sentence using **logical** and appropriate content.

When people claim that they have seen UFOs, a _____ explanation could be

that they actually saw _____ .

Your Turn **Work independently** to complete the sentence using **logical** and appropriate content.

There are a number of _____ arguments for starting high school at 9:00 a.m.,

such as the fact that teenagers _____ .

Be an Academic Author **Work independently** to write two sentences. In your first sentence, use **logical** with a *singular noun* and include a word partner. In your second sentence, use **logical** with a *plural noun*.

❶ _____

_____

❷ _____

_____

> ### grammar tip
> An adjective usually comes before the noun it describes.
> a <u>logical</u> reason
> a <u>green</u> jacket

Write an Academic Paragraph **Complete** the paragraph using **logical** and original content.

English is a challenging language to learn because it doesn't always follow

_____ patterns. For example, most words in Spanish
❶

are easy to pronounce because the letters of the alphabet usually only have one

_____ . However, in English, spelling and pronunciation patterns
❷

_____ significantly. One example is the word "tough," which is spelled
❸

with a "gh" at the end instead of _____ . The "gh" combination can
❹

also be confusing because its pronunciation _____ depending
❺

on whether it comes at the beginning or end of a word. Exceptions like these are very

_____ to students because they seem completely illogical! Nevertheless,
❻

with time and practice, the patterns of English will seem _____ .
❼

maximum
adjective

▶ **Say it:** **max** • i • mum   **Write it:** _____

Meaning	Example
the largest amount of something that is possible	The little girl wanted to ride the _____, but it had already reached **maximum** _____ .
Synonym: most **Antonym:** minimum	

Family

- **Noun:** maximum
- **Verb:** maximize

Word Partners

- _____ amount of — The **maximum amount of** sugar that doctors recommend eating daily is 40 grams.
- _____ length — The **maximum length** that your research paper can be is ten pages.
- _____ number of — The **maximum number of** students that can go on the field trip is 25.

Verbal Practice

Talk about It **Read** each sentence and **think** about how you would complete it.

Discuss your idea with your partner using the sentence frame.

Listen carefully to your partner's and classmates' ideas.

Write your favorite idea in the blank.

❶ If you drive over the **maximum** speed limit, you might get

_____ .

❷ The **maximum** amount of time that I spend on my homework each night is

_____ .

Writing Practice

Collaborate   **Work with your partner** to complete the sentence using **maximum** and appropriate content.

If a student is caught painting graffiti on school grounds, the _____

penalty should be _____ .

Your Turn   **Work independently** to complete the sentence using **maximum** and appropriate content.

The _____ length of time that I could survive without a computer, TV,

or cell phone is probably _____ .

Be an Academic Author   **Work independently** to write two sentences. In your first sentence, use **maximum** with the word partner *maximum length*. In your second sentence, use **maximum** with the word partner *maximum number of*.

❶ _____

_____

❷ _____

_____

> ### grammar tip
>
> *Amount of* and *number of* are quantifiers used to describe how much or how many of a noun there is. Use *amount of* with non-count nouns, and use *number of* with count nouns.
>
> The maximum **amount of time** you have is one hour.
>
> The maximum **number of slices** per person is two.

Write an Academic Paragraph   **Complete** the paragraph using **maximum** and original content.

One summer _____ ❶ _____ that many people

enjoy is going to an amusement park. Kids and adults alike love

the exciting roller coasters and _____ ❷ _____ . While these attractions are

designed to be entertaining, amusement parks are also very _____ ❸ _____

about safety. Most amusement parks follow guidelines established by state and

local governments to keep people safe. For example, many rides have minimum and

_____ ❹ _____ height requirements that are posted next to the entrance. If

you are shorter than the minimum height or taller than the maximum height, you are not

allowed to _____ ❺ _____ . Some rides also have weight restrictions where a

_____ ❻ _____ weight is posted. These safety _____ ❼ _____

are important for keeping riders safe so they can sit back and enjoy the ride.

minimum
adjective

Academic Vocabulary Toolkit

Meaning	Example	
the smallest amount of something that is possible	The **minimum** _____ limit on this highway is _____ miles per hour.	SPEED LIMIT **75** MINIMUM **40**
Synonym: least **Antonym:** maximum		

Family

- **Noun:** minimum
- **Verb:** minimize
- **Adjective:** minimal
- **Adverb:** minimally

Word Partners

- _____ age
- _____ amount of
- _____ requirement

The **minimum age** for buying a video game that is rated "Mature" is 17.

The **minimum amount of** time I am supposed to practice the piano each week is 30 minutes.

If you want to pass this class, the **minimum requirements** are turning in all of your homework and participating every day.

Verbal Practice

Talk about It   **Read** each sentence and **think** about how you would complete it.

Discuss your idea with your partner using the sentence frame.

Listen carefully to your partner's and classmates' ideas.

Write your favorite idea in the blank.

❶ The **minimum** number of classes that I have to take each year is

_____ .

❷ Some stores and restaurants require a **minimum** purchase of

_____ before they'll let you use a debit or credit card.

Writing Practice

Collaborate **Work with your partner** to complete the sentence using **minimum** and appropriate content.

I think the _____ age that people should be before they start working

is _____ because _____ .

Your Turn **Work independently** to complete the sentence using **minimum** and appropriate content.

On school days, I wake up at _____ because the _____

amount of time I need to get ready in the morning is _____ minutes.

Be an Academic Author **Work independently** to write two sentences. In your first sentence, use **minimum** with the word partner *minimum age*. In your second sentence, use **minimum** with the word partner *minimum amount of*.

❶ _____

_____

❷ _____

_____

> **grammar tip**
>
> *Amount of* is a quantifier used to describe how much of a noun there is. Use *amount of* with non-count nouns.
>
> The minimum **amount of time** I spend watching TV every day is 30 minutes.

Write an Academic Paragraph **Complete** the paragraph using **minimum** and original content.

Sleep provides a number of restorative _____ , but most people

❶

still don't get enough of it. The _____ amount of sleep that each

❷

person should get every night varies by age, but, in general, the younger you are, the more

sleep you need. Children in elementary school need a minimum of nine to eleven hours, while

teenagers _____ approximately nine to ten hours a night. Adults

❸

need the _____ , from seven to eight hours. The disadvantages of

❹

sleep deficiency become _____ after just one night of poor rest. In

❺

the short term, sleep deficiency can _____ cognitive impairments and

❻

hallucinations. In the long term, it can put you at risk for heart disease or diabetes. Make sure

you take the time to get the _____ amount of sleep you need in order

❼

to feel and perform at your best.

objective
adjective

Write it: _____

Academic Vocabulary Toolkit

Meaning	Example
based on facts instead of feelings **Synonyms:** fair, neutral, impartial **Antonym:** subjective	The judges wore blindfolds during the _____ so that they would remain **objective** when making their _____ .

Family

- **Noun:** objectivity
- **Adverb:** objectively

Word Partners

• completely _____	I try to be **completely objective** when listening to different political viewpoints.
• _____ decision	Supreme Court justices consider a case and make an **objective decision** based on the Constitution.
• remain _____	Bobby **remained objective** when choosing the basketball team starters, passing over two of his friends for better players.

Verbal Practice

Talk about It **Read** each sentence and **think** about how you would complete it.

Discuss your idea with your partner using the sentence frame.

Listen carefully to your partner's and classmates' ideas.

Write your favorite idea in the blank.

❶ A good _____ always tries to remain **objective**.

❷ It's difficult to be **objective** when writing about a topic that you feel strongly about, such as _____ .

Writing Practice

Collaborate   **Work with your partner** to complete the sentence using **objective** and appropriate content.

If you want to find _____ information about an issue, you should try looking

at resources such as _____ rather than _____ .

Your Turn   **Work independently** to complete the sentence using **objective** and appropriate content.

An _____ review of my locker would reveal that I am _____ .

Be an Academic Author   **Work independently** to write two sentences. In your first sentence, use **objective** with the word partner *completely objective*. In your second sentence, use **objective** with the word partner *remain objective*.

❶ _____

_____

❷ _____

_____

> ### grammar tip
> Adverbs often modify verbs, but they sometimes modify adjectives.
>
> Judges must be **completely objective**.
>
> He likes **really big** dogs.

Write an Academic Paragraph   **Complete** the paragraph using **objective** and original content.

It's essential for scientific research and analysis to remain _____ ❶

and not be influenced by biased organizations or people. A recent example shows the

dangers that can result if researchers do not remain _____ ❷ . In

1998, Dr. Andrew Wakefield published reports linking childhood vaccinations to autism.

Many people _____ ❸ his conclusions and decided not to vaccinate

their children. However, by 2010, other experts _____ ❹ that many

of Dr. Wakefield's results were fabricated and that his study had been funded by a law firm

that hoped to sue the pharmaceutical industry for a lot of _____ ❺ .

This deception put unvaccinated children at risk of _____ ❻

deadly diseases and demonstrates the importance of investigating who funds scientific

_____ ❼ and whether the results have been verified independently.

objectively
adverb

▶ **Say it:** ob • **jec** • tive • ly   **Write it:** _____

Academic Vocabulary Toolkit

Meaning	Example
in a way that is based on facts instead of feelings **Synonyms:** fairly, impartially **Antonym:** subjectively	Before we vote for new student _____ members, we need to assess all the _____ **objectively**.

Family

- **Noun:** objectivity
- **Adjective:** objective

Word Partners

• look at something _____	Police officers must **look at evidence objectively** while investigating a case.
• _____ speaking	**Objectively speaking**, Barack Obama is a skilled orator.
• think _____	Teachers should **think objectively** when assigning final grades.

Verbal Practice

Talk about It   **Read** each sentence and **think** about how you would complete it.

Discuss your idea with your partner using the sentence frame.

Listen carefully to your partner's and classmates' ideas.

Write your favorite idea in the blank.

❶ It's hard to think **objectively** about people who are close to you, such as

your _____ .

❷ **Objectively** speaking, _____ is a talented musician.

Writing Practice

Collaborate **Work with your partner** to complete the sentence using **objectively** and appropriate content.

Parents should not serve as judges in a _____ if their children are participating

because they won't be able to consider all of the performances _____ .

Your Turn **Work independently** to complete the sentence using **objectively** and appropriate content.

_____ speaking, _____ is a well-made movie,

although I personally didn't enjoy it .

Be an Academic Author **Work independently** to write two sentences. In your first sentence, use **objectively** with the word partner *think objectively*. In your second sentence, use **objectively** with the word partner *look at something objectively*.

❶ _____

_____

❷ _____

_____

> ### grammar tip
>
> **Many adverbs describe how something is done. These adverbs often end in *–ly*.**
>
> It's important to **think** <u>objectively</u>.
>
> He **answered** <u>quickly</u>.

Write an Academic Paragraph **Complete** the paragraph using **objectively** and original content.

Some disagreements become so intense that people refuse to _____ ❶

to each other or reconcile. In these instances, it is difficult to resolve the argument because neither

person can see the situation _____ ❷ . When this happens, sometimes

a third person who is not involved in the _____ ❸ , called a mediator,

intervenes to help both parties come to an agreement. Mediators _____ ❹

analyze each party's point of view and the events leading up to the argument. Because the

mediator is objective, and therefore does not _____ ❺ with either party, it is

easier for him or her to find a potential solution. Sometimes mediators are professionals who assist

in legal _____ ❻ , and other times a mediator is a teacher or relative who

helps two friends resolve an argument. Whatever the situation, mediators can help two people

understand each other's points of view and _____ ❼ .

opinion
noun

▶ **Say it:** o • **pin** • ion   *Write it:* _____

Meaning	Example
what someone thinks or believes **Synonym:** belief	In my **opinion**, the pie was _____, but Sherry hated it.

Forms	Family
• **Singular:** opinion • **Plural:** opinions	• **Adjective:** opinionated

Word Partners

• ask for an _____	My best friend wasn't sure whether she wanted to paint her bedroom blue or yellow, so she **asked for my opinion.**
• express an _____	Our teacher had us research a controversial issue and **express an opinion** about it in an essay.
• in my _____	**In my opinion**, the best sport is hockey.

Verbal Practice

Talk about It   **Read** each sentence and **think** about how you would complete it.

Discuss your idea with your partner using the sentence frame.

Listen carefully to your partner's and classmates' ideas.

Write your favorite idea in the blank.

❶ In my **opinion**, all schools should have _____ .

❷ I have a high **opinion** of _____ because _____ is making the world a better place.

Writing Practice

Collaborate **Work with your partner** to complete the sentence using the correct form of **opinion** and appropriate content.

Many teenagers form their _____ by listening to their _____

and reading _____ .

Your Turn **Work independently** to complete the sentence using the correct form of **opinion** and appropriate content.

The best movie of all time, in my _____ , is _____ because

it has _____ .

Be an Academic Author **Work independently** to write two sentences. In your first sentence, use **opinion** in the *plural form*. In your second sentence, use **opinion** in the *singular form* and include a word partner.

❶ _____

_____

❷ _____

_____

> ### grammar tip
>
> **Count nouns name things that can be counted. Count nouns have two forms, singular and plural. To make most count nouns plural, add –s.**
>
> She has strong opinions.
>
> He likes board games.

Write an Academic Paragraph **Complete** the paragraph using the correct form of **opinion** and original content.

Newspapers are excellent _____ for finding information and facts.
                                                    ❶

However, many newspapers also feature a section called the op-ed page in which readers

contribute their _____ on current events and issues. Originally, the op-ed
                                    ❷

page only featured the _____ of individual newspaper staff writers,
                                      ❸

but today, op-ed pages _____ editorials from writers from all over the
                                      ❹

world. In many larger newspapers such as *The New York Times* and _____ ,
                                                                                              ❺

experts and well-known figures often contribute to the op-ed page, but anyone can submit

a letter. If you have a strong _____ about an issue, you should
                                            ❻

write to your local newspaper. If your letter is printed, you might end up influencing the

_____ of other people as well.
          ❼

perspective
noun

▶ **Say it:** per • **spec** • tive   **Write it:** _____

Academic Vocabulary Toolkit

Meaning	Example
the way someone sees or thinks about something	When you have an _____ with a friend, you should try to see the _____ from his or her **perspective**.
Synonym: point of view	

Forms

- *Singular:* perspective
- *Plural:* perspectives

Word Partners

• different _____	Jamal and I have **different perspectives** on the issue of global warming.
• from (my/your/his/her/our/their) _____	The governor is considering reducing schools' budgets, but **from my perspective**, we should give schools more funding.
• unique _____	Artists have a **unique perspective** on street graffiti.

Verbal Practice

Talk about It   **Read** each sentence and **think** about how you would complete it.

Discuss your idea with your partner using the sentence frame.

Listen carefully to your partner's and classmates' ideas.

Write your favorite idea in the blank.

❶ People often write letters and e-mails to newspapers and magazines to give their

perspectives on _____ .

❷ A person with international travel experience has a unique **perspective** on

_____ .

Writing Practice

Collaborate **Work with your partner** to complete the sentence using the correct form of **perspective** and appropriate content.

My activity partner and I have different _____ on the issue of

_____ .

Your Turn **Work independently** to complete the sentence using the correct form of **perspective** and appropriate content.

From my _____ , students at this school should have one free hour every day

to _____ .

Be an Academic Author **Work independently** to write two sentences. In your first sentence, use **perspective** in the *singular form* and include a word partner. In your second sentence, use **perspective** in the *plural form*.

❶ _____

_____

❷ _____

_____

> ### grammar tip
> Count nouns name things that can be counted. Count nouns have two forms, singular and plural. To make most count nouns plural, add –*s*.
>
> We have different perspective**s** on life.
>
> She has some question**s**.

Write an Academic Paragraph **Complete** the paragraph using the correct form of **perspective** and original content.

Parents and teenagers often have trouble seeing things from each other's

_____ ❶ . For example, many teenagers complain that their parents

are too _____ ❷ about issues like curfews or homework. From a

teenager's _____ ❸ , parents should trust their children and give

them more freedom. However, from a parent's perspective, teenagers need lots of

_____ ❹ so that they will grow up to be responsible adults. Although

each of these _____ ❺ is valid, parents and teenagers often end up

_____ ❻ with each other. What can parents and teenagers do to gain

a better understanding of each other's _____ ❼ ?

persuade
verb

Meaning	Example
to convince someone to do or believe something	The girl **persuaded** her parents to adopt a _____ from the animal shelter.
Synonym: influence *Antonym:* dissuade	

Forms		Family
Present: I/You/We/They persuade He/She/It persuades *Past:* persuaded		• *Noun:* persuasion • *Adjective:* persuasive • *Adverb:* persuasively

Word Partners

• attempt to _____	We **attempted to persuade** our coach to end practice early, but she refused.
• fail to _____	Briana **failed to persuade** her sister to give her a ride to school.
• try to _____	Dennis is **trying to persuade** his aunt to give him money to go to the movies tonight.

Verbal Practice

Talk about It   **Read** each sentence and **think** about how you would complete it.

Discuss your idea with your partner using the sentence frame.

Listen carefully to your partner's and classmates' ideas.

Write your favorite idea in the blank.

❶ Sometimes we try to **persuade** our teacher to let us _____.

❷ It can be very difficult to **persuade** young children to eat _____.

Writing Practice

Collaborate **Work with your partner** to complete the sentence using the correct form of **persuade** and appropriate content.

If someone tries to _____ you to do something you don't want to do, one way

to get out of it is to _____ .

Your Turn **Work independently** to complete the sentence using the correct form of **persuade** and appropriate content.

Tracy _____ her teacher to give her more time to do her book report by saying

that _____ .

Be an Academic Author **Work independently** to write two sentences. In your first sentence, use **persuade** in the *simple past tense*. In your second sentence, use **persuade** with the word partner *try to persuade*.

❶ _____

_____

❷ _____

_____

> ## grammar tip
> **To make the simple past tense of regular verbs, add –*ed* or –*d*.**
>
> He persuade**d** me to go.
> We play**ed** tennis today.

Write an Academic Paragraph **Complete** the paragraph using the correct form of **persuade** and original content.

Most people have found themselves in a situation where someone tries to

_____ them to do something they don't want to do.
❶

Sometimes it can be _____ to tell someone "no," especially if
❷

he or she is a _____ or someone you know from school. What
❸

are some _____ for dealing with peer pressure? If someone
❹

attempts to _____ you to do something dangerous or illegal,
❺

you should get out of the situation immediately. Walk away, tell them "no thanks," or ask

a _____ to come over as a distraction. You are an independent
❻

person—don't let anyone _____ you to do something you don't
❼

want to do.

137

persuasion
noun

▶ **Say it:** per • **sua** • sion   *Write it:* _____

<table>
<tr><td colspan="2" align="center">**Academic Vocabulary Toolkit**</td></tr>
<tr><td align="center">**Meaning**</td><td align="center">**Example**</td></tr>
<tr><td>the act of convincing someone to do or believe something</td><td>My friend Alex didn't want to see an _____ movie, but after some **persuasion**, I _____ him.</td></tr>
</table>

Family

- *Verb:* persuade
- *Adjective:* persuasive
- *Adverb:* persuasively

Word Partners

- open to _____   I have never eaten duck before, but I am **open to persuasion**.
- powers of _____   The drama teacher used her **powers of persuasion** to convince Sam to audition for the school play.

Verbal Practice

Talk about It **Read** each sentence and **think** about how you would complete it.

Discuss your idea with your partner using the sentence frame.

Listen carefully to your partner's and classmates' ideas.

Write your favorite idea in the blank.

❶ Many shoppers require a lot of **persuasion** before they will buy

_____ .

❷ Teachers often try to use **persuasion** to convince students that

topics like _____ are relevant to their lives.

Writing Practice

Collaborate   **Work with your partner** to complete the sentence using **persuasion** and appropriate content.

It would take a lot of _____ to make most kids give up _____

for one week.

Your Turn   **Work independently** to complete the sentence using **persuasion** and appropriate content.

When I have some free time, it doesn't take much _____ to convince me to

_____ .

Be an   **Work independently** to write two sentences. In your first sentence, use **persuasion** with the word
Academic   partner *powers of persuasion*. In your second sentence, use **persuasion** with the word partner *open to*
Author   *persuasion*.

❶ _____

_____

❷ _____

_____

> ### grammar tip
> Non-count nouns name things that can't be counted. Non-count nouns have only one form. Do not add an –*s* to a non-count noun.
>
> She is open to **persuasion**.
>
> The **water** is frozen.

Write an   **Complete** the paragraph using **persuasion** and original content.
Academic
Paragraph   Leaders often have the gift of _____ : the ability to convince people
                                                    ❶

to do or believe in the same things as themselves. For example, when people run for president,

they try to _____ people that their ideas are the best ones for running
            ❷

the country. Many teachers and coaches also have powers of _____ ;
                                                            ❸

these are usually the most respected adults at school who _____ kids
                                                          ❹

to do their best and make _____ choices. However, not every person
                          ❺

is open to _____ . Most people will only listen to people that they
            ❻

respect. The gift of persuasion is a rare ability that takes time to _____
                                                                    ❼

as you learn what motivates other people.

precede
verb

▶ **Say it:** pre • **cede**   *Write it:* _____

Meaning	Example
to happen before something else	A flash of _____ usually **precedes** the sound of thunder during a _____ .

Forms		Family
Present:		• **Noun:** precedent
I/You/We/They	precede	• **Adjective:** preceding
He/She/It	precedes	
Past:	preceded	

Word Partners
• immediately _____   A book's table of contents **immediately precedes** the first chapter.

Verbal Practice

Talk about It   **Read** each sentence and **think** about how you would complete it.

Discuss your idea with your partner using the sentence frame.

Listen carefully to your partner's and classmates' ideas.

Write your favorite idea in the blank.

❶ The word *puzzle* **precedes** the word _____ in the dictionary.

❷ A _____ **preceded** the end of our last class.

Writing Practice

Collaborate **Work with your partner** to complete the sentence using the correct form of **precede** and appropriate content.

A _____ immediately _____ the main text in a book.

Your Turn **Work independently** to complete the sentence using the correct form of **precede** and appropriate content.

My birthday, which is in the month of _____ , _____ my friend

_____ 's birthday in _____ .

Be an Academic Author **Work independently** to write two sentences. In your first sentence, use **precede** in the *simple present tense*. In your second sentence, use **precede** in the *simple past tense*.

❶ _____

_____

❷ _____

_____

> **grammar tip**
>
> To make the simple past tense of regular verbs, add *–ed* or *–d*.
>
> An introduction preced**ed** the talent show.
>
> We play**ed** tennis today.

Write an Academic Paragraph **Complete** the paragraph using the correct form of **precede** and original content.

Small tremors called foreshocks sometimes _____ earthquakes, (❶)

but they are often so faint that no one notices them. If an earthquake occurs underneath

the ocean, a powerful tidal wave called a tsunami can _____ and (❷)

cause terrible destruction, even if there are foreshocks as warning. On March 11, 2011,

Japan experienced a _____ earthquake that registered 9.0 (❸)

on the Richter scale—the largest earthquake in Japan's _____ . (❹)

Because the epicenter was underneath the Pacific Ocean, a devastating tidal wave

immediately _____ the earthquake. Nearly 100 foreshocks (❺)

_____ the earthquake, but they mostly went unnoticed. As a result, (❻)

approximately 20,000 _____ died in the earthquake and tsunami. (❼)

141

predict
verb

▶ **Say it:** pre • **dict**   *Write it:* _____

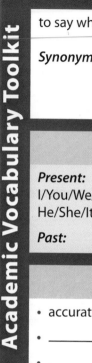
Meaning	Example
to say what will happen in the future	Carlos **predicts** that he
	will become a famous
Synonym: foretell	_____ someday.

Forms		Family
Present:		• **Noun:** prediction
I/You/We/They	predict	• **Adjective:** predictable
He/She/It	predicts	• **Adverb:** predictably
Past:	predicted	

Word Partners

• accurately _____	My mom **accurately predicted** that I would get an A on the test.
• _____ the future	I wish I could **predict the future** and know what will happen in my life.
• _____ the outcome	Harry **predicted the outcome** of the soccer game by saying our team would win 2-1.

Verbal Practice

Talk about It   **Read** each sentence and **think** about how you would complete it.

Discuss your idea with your partner using the sentence frame.

Listen carefully to your partner's and classmates' ideas.

Write your favorite idea in the blank.

❶ Five hundred years ago, no one could have **predicted** the invention of

_____ .

❷ I **predict** that most of my classmates will _____ in the

next five years.

Writing Practice

Collaborate — Work with your partner to complete the sentence using the correct form of **predict** and appropriate content.

I _____ that by 2050, most people will no longer _____ .

Instead, they will _____ .

Your Turn — Work independently to complete the sentence using the correct form of **predict** and appropriate content.

My family has _____ that I will become a _____ .

Be an Academic Author — Work independently to write two sentences. In your first sentence, use **predict** in the *present perfect tense*. In your second sentence, use **predict** in the *simple past tense* and include a word partner.

❶ _____

_____

❷ _____

_____

> ### grammar tip
>
> The present perfect tense is formed with *has/have* + the past participle form of the verb. To make the past participle of regular verbs, add *–ed* or *–d*.
>
> I <u>have predict**ed**</u> the winner.
>
> She <u>has receiv**ed**</u> a letter.

Write an Academic Paragraph — **Complete** the paragraph using the correct form of **predict** and original content.

Predicting the _____ has always been a part of human
❶

existence. Since ancient times, people have employed a number of methods to

_____ the future, some of which are still used today. Some of the
❷

earliest _____ of prediction involved natural phenomena. For
❸

example, Roman priests observed the patterns of flying birds to _____
❹

whether an upcoming event would be successful. Over time, humans developed tools to use

in fortune telling, _____ tarot cards and crystal balls. In fact, tarot cards
❺

are still one of the most _____ tools used for fortune telling today.
❻

While methods for predicting the future have evolved over millennia, one thing has remained

constant: people's desire to _____ into the unknowable future.
❼

prediction
noun

▶ **Say it:** pre • **dic** • tion   **Write it:** _____

Meaning	Example	
a statement about what will happen in the future	During a presidential _____ , TV reporters often make **predictions** about who will _____ .	

Forms	Family
• *Singular:* prediction • *Plural:* predictions	• *Verb:* predict • *Adjective:* predictable • *Adverb:* predictably

Word Partners

• accurate _____	The weather forecaster made an **accurate prediction** about the weather this morning.
• make a _____	Can you **make a prediction** about what will happen next in the story?

Verbal Practice

Talk about It **Read** each sentence and **think** about how you would complete it.

Discuss your idea with your partner using the sentence frame.

Listen carefully to your partner's and classmates' ideas.

Write your favorite idea in the blank.

❶ The latest **prediction** in celebrity gossip is that _____ will get engaged to _____ .

❷ When I make **predictions** about _____ , I am usually right.

Writing Practice

Collaborate **Work with your partner** to complete the sentence using the correct form of **prediction** and appropriate content.

One _____ I can confidently make about our class this month is that we will

have to _____ .

Your Turn **Work independently** to complete the sentence using the correct form of **prediction** and appropriate content.

When people make _____ about the future of the planet, I usually

_____ attention because I think that _____ .

Be an Academic Author **Work independently** to write two sentences. In your first sentence, use **prediction** in the *singular form*. In your second sentence, use **prediction** in the *plural form* and include a word partner.

❶ _____

_____

❷ _____

_____

> ### grammar tip
>
> Count nouns name things that can be counted. Count nouns have two forms, singular and plural. To make most count nouns plural, add *–s*.
>
> My predictions were accurate.
>
> He likes board games.

Write an Academic Paragraph **Complete** the paragraph using the correct form of **prediction** and original content.

Weather forecasting is the use of technology to make _____
❶

about the weather. In the past, people used instruments called barometers to

_____ pressure in the atmosphere and make weather
❷

_____ . This information was _____ to sailors
❸   ❹

and farmers, whose work (and lives) often depended on accurate weather forecasts. Today,

meteorologists use a wide range of sophisticated technology to _____
❺

the weather. Contemporary methods include using forecast models and the Analog

technique, which _____ algorithms and information from satellites to
❻

provide weather predictions. These methods allow forecasters to make daily and long-term

_____ about the weather.
❼

145

previous
adjective

▶ **Say it:** **pre** · vi · ous   **Write it:** _____

<table>
<tr><th colspan="2">Meaning</th><th>Example</th></tr>
<tr><td colspan="2">happening before something else

Synonym: prior</td><td>Greg didn't _____

well the **previous** night

because a car _____

kept waking him up.</td></tr>
</table>

Academic Vocabulary Toolkit

Family
• **Adverb:** previously

Word Partners	
• _____ day/night/ week/month/year	It's been sunny and warm this week, but the **previous week** was rainy and cold.
• _____ experience	My **previous experience** with children includes babysitting and working as a summer camp counselor.

Verbal Practice

Talk about It **Read** each sentence and **think** about how you would complete it.

Discuss your idea with your partner using the sentence frame.

Listen carefully to your partner's and classmates' ideas.

Write your favorite idea in the blank.

❶ In the **previous** chapter of our science textbook, we learned

about _____ .

❷ I was able to purchase this _____ for a great price because

the **previous** owner had to move.

Writing Practice

Collaborate   **Work with your partner** to complete the sentence using **previous** and appropriate content.

This year I'm going to _____ more than I have in _____ years.

Your Turn   **Work independently** to complete the sentence using **previous** and appropriate content.

This school is different than my _____ school because the students

are _____ .

Be an Academic Author   **Work independently** to write two sentences. In your first sentence, use **previous** with a *singular noun*. In your second sentence, use **previous** with the word partner *previous day/night/week/month/year*.

❶ _____

_____

❷ _____

_____

> **grammar tip**
>
> **An adjective usually comes before the noun it describes.**
>
> the <u>previous</u> week
>
> a <u>big</u> house
>
> a <u>green</u> jacket

Write an Academic Paragraph   **Complete** the paragraph using **previous** and original content.

Today, newborn babies _____ ❶ top medical care. However, in _____ ❷ decades, this wasn't always the case. Previously, when a baby appeared sick or _____ ❸ at birth, doctors would leave the baby alone and see if he or she _____ ❹ . Then, in 1952, physician Virginia Apgar _____ ❺ a test to evaluate the health of newborn babies based on five factors: Appearance, Pulse, Grimace, Activity, and Respiration (APGAR). The APGAR test revolutionized the way doctors _____ ❻ babies. Physicians became more proactive about monitoring babies' _____ ❼ , even competing with other doctors to get the best scores for their newborn patients! Hospitals around the United States quickly adopted the APGAR test because it was superior to _____ ❽ methods for evaluating newborns. As a result, most babies are tested at birth using the APGAR scale.

previously
adverb

Academic Vocabulary Toolkit

Meaning	Example	
at an earlier time	Amy **previously** worked as a _____ ; now she works in an _____ shop.	
Synonym: before		

Family

- *Adjective:* previous

Word Partners

• _____ described	Reporters **previously described** the crime as an accident, but it turned out to be intentional.
• _____ mentioned	As I **previously mentioned** in my blog entry, I'd love to see everyone at my birthday party this weekend.
• _____ worked	Only people who have **previously worked** as technicians will be considered for the job.

Verbal Practice

Talk about It **Read** each sentence and **think** about how you would complete it.

Discuss your idea with your partner using the sentence frame.

Listen carefully to your partner's and classmates' ideas.

Write your favorite idea in the blank.

❶ You **previously** mentioned where the best place to buy _____ is, but I've forgotten.

❷ My friend tried to introduce me to _____ , but we had **previously** met.

148

Writing Practice

Collaborate **Work with your partner** to complete the sentence using **previously** and appropriate content.

One way to remember where you _____ stopped reading in a book is

to _____ .

Your Turn **Work independently** to complete the sentence using **previously** and appropriate content.

_____ on the TV show _____ , two of the main characters

_____ .

Be an Academic Author **Work independently** to write two sentences. In your first sentence, use **previously** with the word partner *previously mentioned*. In your second sentence, use **previously** with the word partner *previously worked*.

❶ _____

_____

❷ _____

_____

> ### grammar tip
> Many adverbs go after the main verb, but some come before.
>
> Do you remember the store I **previously mentioned**?
>
> She **really likes** dogs.

Write an Academic Paragraph **Complete** the paragraph using **previously** and original content.

Commercial airline travel has evolved considerably over the last few decades.

_____ , it took days, weeks, or even months for travelers to reach
                    ❶

far-off _____ . But with the invention of _____ ,
          ❷   **❸**

travelers can now cross oceans and _____ distances in a matter of
                                      ❹

hours. The first commercial flights were offered in the early 1900s, but the first transatlantic

flights weren't _____ until 1945. Back then, a flight from Boston to
                  ❺

London _____ more than 15 hours, while today it takes a little more
          ❻

than six! Airline travel was _____ considered a luxury, but now it
                              ❼

is a quick, affordable travel option for most people. Each year, there are over 600 million

_____ who fly on commercial airlines in the United States.
  ❽

prioritize
verb

Say it: pri • **or** • i • tize   **Write it:** _____

Meaning	Example
to decide what tasks are most important so you can do those first	In an _____ room, nurses have to **prioritize** who the _____ will take care of first.

Forms	Family
Present: I/You/We/They prioritize He/She/It prioritizes **Past:** prioritized	• **Noun:** priority

Word Partners

• need to _____	The band **needs to prioritize** practicing for the holiday concert before anything else.
• _____ a task	We have very little time and a lot to do, so we must **prioritize our tasks**.

Verbal Practice

Talk about It   **Read** each sentence and **think** about how you would complete it.

Discuss your idea with your partner using the sentence frame.

Listen carefully to your partner's and classmates' ideas.

Write your favorite idea in the blank.

❶ If you want to **prioritize** your tasks, you should probably finish your homework before you _____ .

❷ One person who can help you **prioritize** your responsibilities is _____ .

Writing Practice

Collaborate **Work with your partner** to complete the sentence using the correct form of **prioritize** and appropriate content.

When I have a lot of homework for my classes, I _____ which assignments to

do first by deciding which _____ .

Your Turn **Work independently** to complete the sentence using the correct form of **prioritize** and appropriate content.

I _____ spending time with my _____ before anyone else

because _____ .

Be an Academic Author **Work independently** to write two sentences. In your first sentence, use **prioritize** in the *simple present tense*. In your second sentence, use **prioritize** in the *simple past tense*.

❶ _____

_____

❷ _____

_____

> **grammar tip**
>
> **To make the simple past tense of regular verbs, add –ed or –d.**
>
> Ralph prioritiz**ed** his tasks for the party.
>
> I play**ed** tennis today.

Write an Academic Paragraph **Complete** the paragraph using the correct form of **prioritize** and original content.

During an emergency, it can be difficult to _____ what you should
                                                      ❶

do. For example, what injuries need to be addressed _____ , and
                                                              ❷

which can wait? When you find yourself in a life-threatening emergency such as a fire or

_____ , your priority should be to get out of the situation as quickly
        ❸

as possible. Once you are somewhere safe, call 911 and then _____
                                                                    ❹

any injuries to yourself or others around you. It's important to _____
                                                                        ❺

severe injuries to the head or chest before any others as those are life threatening. If someone

is unconscious, _____ the person on his or her side and cover the
                        ❻

person with a blanket. If you _____ your needs in an emergency, you
                                    ❼

will be able to react calmly and effectively until help arrives.

priority
noun

Say it: pri • **or** • i • ty

Write it: _____

Academic Vocabulary Toolkit

Meaning	Example	
the most important thing you have to do or give attention to before everything else	On an airplane, _____ is the top **priority**.	

Forms	Family
• *Singular:* priority • *Plural:* priorities	• *Verb:* prioritize

Word Partners	
• give _____ to something	Congress's new budget **gives priority to** education programs.
• high/top _____	Ralph cares a lot about his grades, so studying is a **high priority** for him.
• place _____ on something	Our teacher **places priority** on us trying our hardest in class.

Verbal Practice

Talk about It **Read** each sentence and **think** about how you would complete it.

Discuss your idea with your partner using the sentence frame.

Listen carefully to your partner's and classmates' ideas.

Write your favorite idea in the blank.

❶ Restaurants often say that their top **priority** is to give customers

_____ .

❷ Most teenagers' **priorities** are _____ and

_____ .

Writing Practice

Collaborate **Work with your partner** to complete the sentence using the correct form of **priority** and appropriate content.

If I moved to a new town or city, finding a _____ would be a high

_____ for me.

Your Turn **Work independently** to complete the sentence using the correct form of **priority** and appropriate content.

I care a lot about my _____ , so I give top _____ to activities

like _____ .

Be an Academic Author **Work independently** to write two sentences. In your first sentence, use **priority** in the *plural form*. In your second sentence, use **priority** in the *singular form* and include a word partner.

❶ _____

_____

❷ _____

_____

> ## grammar tip
>
> To form the plural of a noun that ends in a consonant + *y*, change the *y* to *i* and add *–es*.
>
> priority—priorities
>
> puppy—puppies

Write an Academic Paragraph **Complete** the paragraph using the correct form of **priority** and original content.

Gardening is a fun activity that can yield beautiful flowers and tasty

_____ . To start a garden, you will have to consider the
　　　　❶

different _____ for growing plants. First, sunlight is the top
　　　　　　　❷

_____ for most fruits and vegetables. Many plants, such as tomatoes
　　　❸

and peppers, _____ six or more hours of full sun every day. However, for
　　　　　　❹

other plants, such as beans and lettuce, sunlight isn't as high of a _____ ;
　　　　　　　　　　　　　　　　　　　　　❺

they can grow with only a few hours of sun a day. Another _____ for
　　　　　　　　　　　　　　　　❻

starting a garden is protecting plants from insects and animals. Many gardeners put wire fences

around their gardens to _____ hungry intruders and use natural
　　　　　　　　❼

pesticides to discourage insects. Keeping these priorities in mind will help you create a beautiful

and bountiful garden.

produce
verb

Say it: pro • **duce**   *Write it:* _____

Academic Vocabulary Toolkit

Meaning	Example
to create something *Synonym:* make	California and Florida **produce** most of the _____ grown in the United States.

Forms

Present:

I/You/We/They	produce
He/She/It	produces

Past: produced

Family

- *Nouns:* product, production, producer
- *Adjective:* productive
- *Adverb:* productively

Word Partners

- ability to _____ — People with Type 1 diabetes do not have the **ability to produce** insulin on their own.

- _____ results — Did your experiment **produce results** that support your hypothesis?

Verbal Practice

Talk about It **Read** each sentence and **think** about how you would complete it.

Discuss your idea with your partner using the sentence frame.

Listen carefully to your partner's and classmates' ideas.

Write your favorite idea in the blank.

❶ A factory that makes car parts might **produce** windshield wipers or _____ .

❷ In this class, we have **produced** _____ and _____ for assignments.

Writing Practice

Collaborate **Work with your partner** to complete the sentence using the correct form of **produce** and appropriate content.

In recent years, technology companies have _____ incredible inventions,

such as _____ .

Your Turn **Work independently** to complete the sentence using the correct form of **produce** and appropriate content.

Our science experiment _____ a huge _____ .

Be an **Work independently** to write two sentences. In your first sentence, use **produce** in the *present perfect*
Academic *tense.* In your second sentence, use **produce** in the *simple past tense.*
Author

❶ _____

_____

❷ _____

_____

> ## grammar tip
>
> **The present perfect tense is formed with *has/have* + the past participle form of the verb. To make the past participle of regular verbs, add *–ed* or *–d*.**
>
> Their farm <u>has produc**ed**</u> apples this year.
>
> We <u>have start**ed**</u> to pack for our trip.

Write an **Complete** the paragraph using the correct form of **produce** and original
Academic content.
Paragraph

In many countries outside of the United States, families _____
❶

the food that they eat themselves. For instance, people in rural areas often grow their

own _____ and raise animals, such as chickens, sheep, and
❷

_____ . To help these farmers thrive, some organizations provide
❸

small loans of less than a hundred dollars called micro-loans. These loans do not provide very

much money, but in _____ countries, small amounts of money can
❹

make a significant difference for struggling families. For example, a micro-loan might help

a family buy an extra goat. When the goat _____ milk, the family
❺

can sell the milk or make dairy products, such as _____ . Over time,
❻

the family can make extra money to repay the loan, buy farm equipment, and send their

_____ to school.
❼

product
noun

▶ **Say it:** **prod** · uct   *Write it:* _____

Academic Vocabulary Toolkit

Meaning	Example	
something that is made or grown *Synonyms:* item, merchandise	This store sells **products** like party hats and _____ .	

Forms	Family
• *Singular:* product • *Plural:* products	• *Verb:* produce • *Adjective:* productive • *Adverb:* productively

Word Partners	
• consumer _____	**Consumer products** are items that people buy for their personal use.
• finished _____	My paper was difficult to write, but after a few rounds of edits, I was happy with the **finished product**.
• sell a _____	My mother **sells stationery products** in her store.

Verbal Practice

Talk about It **Read** each sentence and **think** about how you would complete it.

Discuss your idea with your partner using the sentence frame.

Listen carefully to your partner's and classmates' ideas.

Write your favorite idea in the blank.

❶ An example of a **product** that helps the environment is a

_____ .

❷ A business has to decide on the right _____ for its **products**

in order to be competitive.

156

Writing Practice

Collaborate **Work with your partner** to complete the sentence using the correct form of **product** and appropriate content.

One hair_____ that many teenagers use is _____ .

Your Turn **Work independently** to complete the sentence using the correct form of **product** and appropriate content.

Someday I would like to have a _____ store that sells high-quality

_____ such as _____ .

Be an Academic Author **Work independently** to write two sentences. In your first sentence, use **product** in the *singular form*. In your second sentence, use **product** in the *plural form*.

❶ _____

_____

❷ _____

_____

> ### grammar tip
>
> Count nouns name things that can be counted. Count nouns have two forms, singular and plural. To make most count nouns plural, add –s.
>
> I use recycled products.
>
> He likes board games.

Write an Academic Paragraph **Complete** the paragraph using the correct form of **product** and original content.

An entrepreneur is a person who creates a new _____ or **❶**

business. Entrepreneurs first generate an an idea and then _____ **❷**

a plan for making it a reality. In order to fund their idea, entrepreneurs usually find

investors or get a loan from a _____ . This requires the **❸**

entrepreneur to _____ that their idea will be profitable. One **❹**

way that entrepreneurs accomplish this is to test their _____ **❺**

with a small group and collect feedback. For example, if an entrepreneur wants to

start a cookie business, they might give away their cookies at public events such as

_____ and distribute surveys asking people what they like and dislike **❻**

about the cookies. This process allows entrepreneurs to share positive feedback with investors,

and it can also help them perfect their _____ before they sell it. **❼**

react
verb

► **Say it:** re • **act**   **Write it:** _____

Meaning	Example
to say or do something because of something else that has happened **Synonym:** respond	When Alicia smelled _____ coming from the kitchen, she **reacted** quickly and called _____ .

Academic Vocabulary Toolkit

Forms	Family
Present: I/You/We/They react He/She/It reacts **Past:** reacted	• **Noun:** reaction • **Adjective:** reactive • **Adverb:** reactively

Word Partners

- _____ negatively/positively — When I told my teacher that I forgot my homework, he **reacted negatively** by giving me a zero.
- _____ quickly/slowly — The bus driver **reacted quickly** and swerved to avoid the child who had run into the street.
- slow to _____ — At first everyone was **slow to react** to the fire alarm, but after a minute the students quickly walked out of the classroom.

Verbal Practice

Talk about It **Read** each sentence and **think** about how you would complete it.

Discuss your idea with your partner using the sentence frame.

Listen carefully to your partner's and classmates' ideas.

Write your favorite idea in the blank.

❶ I **reacted** negatively to the news that

_____ .

❷ If there were a fire at school, I would **react** quickly and

_____ .

158

Writing Practice

Collaborate   **Work with your partner** to complete the sentence using the correct form of **react** and appropriate content.

I don't always know how to _____ when people talk to me about serious

subjects like _____ because _____ .

Your Turn   **Work independently** to complete the sentence using the correct form of **react** and appropriate content.

When I am worried about something, I usually _____ by

_____ .

Be an Academic Author   **Work independently** to write two sentences. In your first sentence, use **react** with the adverb of frequency *usually*. In your second sentence, use **react** in the *simple past tense* and include a word partner.

❶ _____

_____

❷ _____

_____

grammar tip

Adverbs of frequency show how often something happens. They usually go before the main verb.

I **usually** **react** to bad news by calling my sister.

He **frequently** **arrives** late to class.

Write an Academic Paragraph   **Complete** the paragraph using the correct form of **react** and original content.

Social psychologists often use experiments to analyze how people _____

❶

to specific situations. One famous study is the Stanford prison experiment

_____ by Philip Zimbardo in 1971. Zimbardo wanted to

❷

_____ the psychological effects of being a prison guard,

❸

so he selected 24 students to live in a mock prison. Students were assigned

_____ as either prisoners or prison guards. The way in

❹

which the participants _____ to the experiment shocked

❺

Zimbardo. Participants who were "prison guards" regularly punished the "prisoners" and

_____ aggressive attitudes. In turn, the "prisoners" reacted with

❻

passive, depressed _____ . Zimbardo quickly stopped the experiment,

❼

but it _____ fascinating insight into human psychology.

❽

reaction

noun

▶ **Say it:** re • **ac** • tion   *Write it:* _____

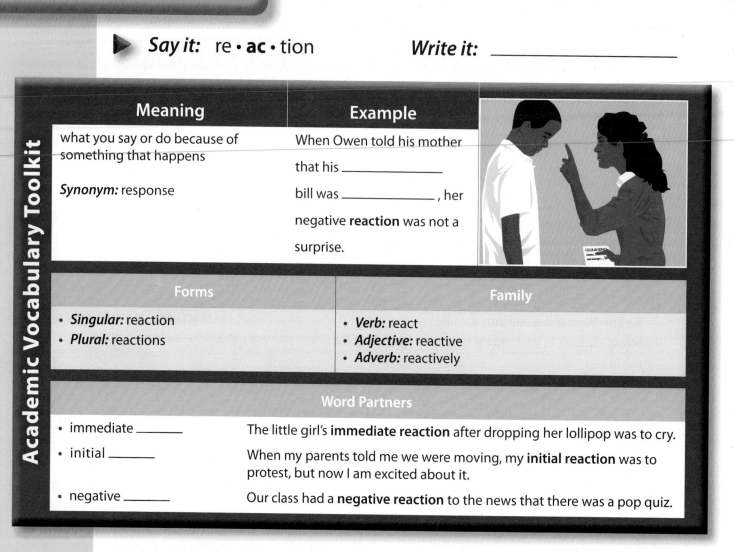

Meaning	Example
what you say or do because of something that happens **Synonym:** response	When Owen told his mother that his _____ bill was _____ , her negative **reaction** was not a surprise.

Forms	Family
• *Singular:* reaction • *Plural:* reactions	• **Verb:** react • **Adjective:** reactive • **Adverb:** reactively

Word Partners	
• immediate _____	The little girl's **immediate reaction** after dropping her lollipop was to cry.
• initial _____	When my parents told me we were moving, my **initial reaction** was to protest, but now I am excited about it.
• negative _____	Our class had a **negative reaction** to the news that there was a pop quiz.

Verbal Practice

Talk about It   **Read** each sentence and **think** about how you would complete it.

Discuss your idea with your partner using the sentence frame.

Listen carefully to your partner's and classmates' ideas.

Write your favorite idea in the blank.

❶ Many people have had negative **reactions** to _____ 's latest song—it's very annoying.

❷ If I stayed out all night, my parents' immediate **reaction** would be to

_____ .

Writing Practice

Collaborate   **Work with your partner** to complete the sentence using the correct form of **reaction** and appropriate content.

On reality shows such as _____ , people like to watch the contestants'

emotional _____ when _____ .

Your Turn   **Work independently** to complete the sentence using the correct form of **reaction** and appropriate content.

If I won the lottery, my initial _____ would probably be to

_____ .

Be an Academic Author   **Work independently** to write two sentences. In your first sentence, use **reaction** in the *plural form*. In your second sentence, use **reaction** in the *singular form* and include a word partner.

❶ _____

_____

❷ _____

_____

> **grammar tip**
>
> **Count nouns name things that can be counted. Count nouns have two forms, singular and plural. To make most count nouns plural, add –s.**
>
> There were mixed reaction**s** to the news.
>
> He likes board game**s**.

Write an Academic Paragraph   **Complete** the paragraph using the correct form of **reaction** and original content.

Natural disasters such as earthquakes and _____ are events
❶

that provoke emotional _____ among the public. One reason for
❷

this is that TV stations and newspapers usually show vivid _____
❸

of people affected by natural disasters. For example, some victims lose their

_____ or even family members. In response, people often react by
❹

donating money or _____ , even if they don't have a connection to the
❺

_____ where a disaster occurred. People also follow the news to see
❻

the government's _____ and how it handles the situation. A natural
❼

disaster is a shocking phenomenon, but it can also bring people together in unexpected ways.

relevance

noun

Say it: **rel** • e • vance   **Write it:** _____

Meaning	Example	
being directly related to a situation or topic **Antonym:** irrelevance	It may not seem like it sometimes, but _____ actually has a lot of **relevance** in our everyday _____ .	59.99 x .20 20%

Family

• **Adjective:** relevant

Word Partners

• direct _____	Earthquakes have **direct relevance** to people living in California.
• particular _____	Air pollution has **particular relevance** for people with asthma.
• personal _____	Classical music has **personal relevance** to me because I want to be a professional pianist.

Verbal Practice

Talk about It   **Read** each sentence and **think** about how you would complete it.

Discuss your idea with your partner using the sentence frame.

Listen carefully to your partner's and classmates' ideas.

Write your favorite idea in the blank.

❶ News reports about snowstorms have little **relevance** for people living

in _____ .

❷ The issue of _____ is of particular **relevance** to young

people because it's something they have to deal with every day.

Writing Practice

Collaborate **Work with your partner** to complete the sentence using **relevance** and appropriate content.

School elections for class officers have direct _____ to me and my classmates

because _____ .

Your Turn **Work independently** to complete the sentence using **relevance** and appropriate content.

One song that has personal _____ to my life is _____

by _____ .

Be an Academic Author **Work independently** to write two sentences. In your first sentence, use **relevance** with the word partner *personal relevance*. In your second sentence, use **relevance** with the word partner *particular relevance*.

❶ _____

_____

❷ _____

_____

> ## grammar tip
> Non-count nouns name things that can't be counted. Non-count nouns have only one form. Do not add an –*s* to a non-count noun.
>
> Your point has no **relevance** to this topic.
>
> The **water** is frozen.

Write an Academic Paragraph **Complete** the paragraph using **relevance** and original content.

Many parents think that computer and video games have no _____❶

to their children's education. However, some researchers _____❷

that these games, in moderation, can have _____❸ effects on

students' confidence levels and their ability to work in groups. For example, some games

_____❹ players to work together to complete challenging tasks, while

other games test kids' problem-solving _____❺ . Whether students

solve a complex logic puzzle by themselves or build an entire new world with a friend, it can

_____❻ their self-esteem substantially. While playing too many computer

and video games can distract students from their academic responsibilities, these games may have

surprising _____❼ to the intellectual and social development of children.

relevant
adjective

Write it: _____

Academic Vocabulary Toolkit

Meaning	Example
directly related to a situation or topic	The _____ is a **relevant** factor for pilots to consider before they _____ .
Synonym: appropriate *Antonym:* irrelevant	

Family

• *Noun:* relevance

Word Partners

• _____ factor — Class participation is a **relevant factor** that teachers consider when calculating students' grades.

• _____ information — When you fill out a scholarship application, you need to provide **relevant information** or it might be rejected.

• _____ issue — The high cost of attending college is a **relevant issue** for high school seniors and their families.

Verbal Practice

Talk about It **Read** each sentence and **think** about how you would complete it.

Discuss your idea with your partner using the sentence frame.

Listen carefully to your partner's and classmates' ideas.

Write your favorite idea in the blank.

❶ Some students say that history isn't **relevant** to their lives, but events like

_____ have impacted everyone in the United States.

❷ You should include **relevant** information such as a _____

on a poster advertising a missing pet.

Writing Practice

Collaborate **Work with your partner** to complete the sentence using **relevant** and appropriate content.

Two _____ factors to consider before you sign up for a field trip

are _____ and _____ .

Your Turn **Work independently** to complete the sentence using **relevant** and appropriate content.

What I am learning in my _____ class right now is _____

to my future career because I want to be _____ .

Be an Academic Author **Work independently** to write two sentences using the word **relevant**. In your first sentence, use **relevant** with a *plural noun*. In your second sentence, use **relevant** with the word partner *relevant information*.

❶ _____

_____

❷ _____

_____

> **grammar tip**
>
> Adjectives do not have plural forms. Do not add an –*s* to adjectives when they describe plural nouns.
>
> <u>relevant</u> factor**s**
>
> <u>loud</u> dog**s**

Write an Academic Paragraph **Complete** the paragraph using **relevant** and original content.

School newspapers are a great way to _____ ❶ the field of journalism

and learn more about local and global issues. Some school newspaper articles are written

about events at school, such as _____ ❷ , which are immediately

_____ ❸ to students. However, student reporters also have to write

about international topics, including environmental or _____ ❹ issues,

and find a way to make these topics _____ ❺ to their classmates.

Global events like wars and elections are still _____ ❻ to students

because the world has become increasingly connected. School newspapers allow student

reporters and readers to learn more about the world and _____ ❼

important issues with their peers.

require
verb

Academic Vocabulary Toolkit

Meanings	Examples
1. to need something	1. Puppies **require** a lot of _____ .
2. to make someone do something	2. Our gym teacher **requires** us to do _____ situps every day.

Forms		Family
Present:		• **Noun:** requirement
I/You/We/They	require	• **Adjective:** required
He/She/It	requires	
Past:	required	

Word Partners

- _____ approval   We **require approval** from a parent or guardian before you can go on the field trip.
- _____ attention   Young children **require attention** at all times.
- _____ effort   This teacher **requires a lot of effort** from his students.

Verbal Practice

Talk about It **Read** each sentence and **think** about how you would complete it.

Discuss your idea with your partner using the sentence frame.

Listen carefully to your partner's and classmates' ideas.

Write your favorite idea in the blank.

❶ Kids **require** a lot of _____ to become healthy and strong.

❷ To sleep well at night, I **require** _____ .

❸ Our teacher **requires** every student in this class to _____ .

❹ At home, my parents **require** me to _____ .

Writing Practice

Collaborate **Work with your partner** to complete the sentence using the correct form of **require** and appropriate content.

Teachers usually _____ students to _____

if they miss a day of school.

Your Turn **Work independently** to complete the sentence using the correct form of **require** and appropriate content.

At my old school, the dress code _____ students to wear

_____ .

Be an Academic Author **Work independently** to write two sentences using Meaning 2 of **require**. In your first sentence, use **require** in the *simple past tense*. In your second sentence, use **require** with the adverb of frequency *usually*.

❶ _____

_____

❷ _____

_____

> **grammar tip**
>
> Adverbs of frequency show how often something happens. They usually go before the main verb.
>
> My parents **usually require** me to do chores.
>
> She **generally doesn't** eat fish.

Write an Academic Paragraph **Complete** the paragraph using the correct form of **require** and original content.

Attendance policies in college are much different than those in high school. First of all, colleges

do not _____ students to report to a homeroom in the morning.
        ❶

In fact, some professors do not even _____ students to be in class
                                     ❷

every day. At many _____ , students only have to complete required
                   ❸

assignments and _____ in order to pass a course. Because teachers do
                ❹

not _____ perfect attendance, students are free to come to class when
    ❺

they choose, which is helpful if students are _____ or have to miss class
                                             ❻

for another reason. Since many college _____ can have hundreds of
                                       ❼

students, it would be impossible for professors to keep track of which students came to class on a

given day.

requirement
noun

Write it: _____

Academic Vocabulary Toolkit

Meanings	Examples
1. something that you need	**1.** Food and _____ are basic **requirements** for humans to live.
2. something that you have to do *Synonyms:* rule, necessity	**2.** Wearing a _____ is a **requirement** if you want to play _____ or softball.

PROTECTIVE GEAR MUST BE WORN DURING GAMES

Forms	Family
• *Singular:* requirement • *Plural:* requirements	• *Verb:* require • *Adjective:* required

Word Partners	
• basic _____	Understanding grammar is a **basic requirement** for studying a language.
• meet a _____	Most models must **meet the requirement** of being 5'9" or taller.
• minimum _____	If you don't meet the **minimum requirements** for this class, you will fail it.

Verbal Practice

Talk about It **Read** each sentence and **think** about how you would complete it.

Discuss your idea with your partner using the sentence frame.

Listen carefully to your partner's and classmates' ideas.

Write your favorite idea in the blank.

❶ Having _____ is a **requirement** for all animals.

❷ If someone has bad eyesight, wearing _____ is a **requirement** for them in order to drive.

❸ Amusement parks often have strict **requirements** about _____ .

❹ One of the main **requirements** for playing a sport at this school is _____ .

Writing Practice

Collaborate   **Work with your partner** to complete the sentence using the correct form of **requirement** and appropriate content.

One _____ for recycling things correctly is _____ .

Your Turn   **Work independently** to complete the sentence using the correct form of **requirement** and appropriate content.

If someone wants to date me, they have to meet the following _____ :

they have to be _____ and _____ .

Be an Academic Author   **Work independently** to write two sentences. In your first sentence, use **requirement** in the *singular form*. In your second sentence, use **requirement** in the *plural form* and include a word partner.

❶ _____

_____

❷ _____

_____

> ## grammar tip
> Count nouns name things that can be counted. Count nouns have two forms, singular and plural. To make most count nouns plural, add –s.
>
> This class has easy requirement**s**.
>
> He likes board game**s**.

Write an Academic Paragraph   **Complete** the paragraph using the correct form of **requirement** and original content.

If you like to travel, you should _____ becoming a flight
❶

attendant. Flight attendants are responsible for the safety and comfort of passengers on

_____ . In order to become a flight attendant, you have to meet a
❷

few _____ . First, a high school diploma is the minimum educational
❸

_____ to work for most airlines, though a college degree is preferred.
❹

Another _____ to be a flight attendant is that you have to keep calm
❺

during emergencies so that you can _____ passengers and give them
❻

instructions. One last _____ is that flight attendants often have to stay
❼

overnight in hotels and be away from their _____ for long periods.
❽

respond
verb

▶ **Say it:** re • **spond**　　　　　　**Write it:** _____

Meanings	Examples	
1. to reply *Synonym:* answer	**1.** When you receive a gift, it is polite to **respond** by saying, "_____."	Thank you!
2. to react because of something that has happened	**2.** After the team lost its second _____ in a row, the star player **responded** by _____ stomping off the field.	

Forms		Family
Present: I/You/We/They　　　　respond He/She/It　　　　responds **Past:**　　　　responded		• **Noun:** response • **Adjective:** responsive

Word Partners

• fail to _____	She **failed to respond** to the special online offer before it expired.
• _____ positively	Taylor **responded positively** to the news that he passed his algebra test.
• quickly _____	Jamal **quickly responded** to his girlfriend's text message.

Verbal Practice

Talk about It　**Read** each sentence and **think** about how you would complete it.

　　　　　　Discuss your idea with your partner using the sentence frame.

　　　　　　Listen carefully to your partner's and classmates' ideas.

　　　　　　Write your favorite idea in the blank.

❶ I don't like it when people **respond** with _____ in an e-mail.

❷ If someone helped me, I would **respond**, "_____."

❸ When a popular band like _____ appears on stage, the audience usually **responds** by _____ .

❹ When I receive a text message from a friend, I generally **respond** within _____ .

Writing Practice

Collaborate **Work with your partner** to complete the sentences using the correct form of **respond** and appropriate content.

❶ The actor failed to _____ to my request for _____ .

❷ If someone talked badly about one of my friends, I would quickly _____

by _____ .

Your Turn **Work independently** to complete the sentences using the correct form of **respond** and appropriate content.

❶ I generally _____ to invitations by _____ .

❷ Teachers _____ positively when students _____ .

Be an Academic Author **Work independently** to write two sentences. In your first sentence, use **respond** with the adverb of frequency *generally*. In your second sentence, use **respond** in the *simple past tense*.

MEANING ❶ _____

_____

MEANING ❷ _____

_____

> **grammar tip**
>
> **Adverbs of frequency show how often something happens. They usually go before the main verb.**
>
> I <u>generally</u> **respond** to text messages right away.
>
> You <u>always</u> **forget** your keys.

Write an Academic Paragraph **Complete** the paragraph using the correct form of **respond** and original content.

Students _____ to the stress of final exams in various ways.
❶

Some students _____ positively to the extra pressure by following
❷

a consistent _____ schedule, sleeping and eating well, and
❸

avoiding distractions like _____ . On the other hand, some students
❹

_____ negatively to exam pressure. Instead of using their free time
❺

wisely, they spend hours _____ instead of studying and come to class
❻

unprepared to tackle an exam. The most productive way to _____ to
❼

exam stress is to study daily, get plenty of sleep, and eat healthy meals and snacks.

response
noun

▶ **Say it:** re · **sponse**   **Write it:** _____

Meanings	Examples	
1. a spoken or written answer	**1.** When Megan asked her _____ if she could stay out until 2:00 a.m., her mother's **response** was, "_____!"	
2. how a person reacts when something happens *Synonym:* reaction	**2.** Mark's _____ **response** to seeing a _____ was to jump onto his desk.	

Forms	Family
• *Singular:* response • *Plural:* responses	• *Verb:* respond • *Adjective:* responsive

Word Partners	
• emotional _____	Our class had an **emotional response** to the news that our teacher was retiring.
• (my/your/his/her/our/their) immediate _____	When Colleen heard some loud thunder from the storm outside, **her immediate response** was to cover her ears.
• positive _____	Kylee had a **positive response** when she won the contest.

Verbal Practice

Talk about It   **Read** each sentence and **think** about how you would complete it.

Discuss your idea with your partner using the sentence frame.

Listen carefully to your partner's and classmates' ideas.

Write your favorite idea in the blank.

❶ A written **response** for class should never include _____ .

❷ An acceptable **response** to "Excuse me" is, "_____."

❸ Some fans had emotional **responses** to the news that _____ died.

❹ My friend _____ in **response** to the surprise birthday party that we threw for her.

response
noun

Writing Practice

Collaborate   **Work with your partner** to complete the sentences using the correct form of **response** and appropriate content.

1. So far Tony has received several _____ to his _____ invitation.

2. I usually expect a positive _____ if I ask a friend to _____ with me.

Your Turn   **Work independently** to complete the sentences using the correct form of **response** and appropriate content.

1. Making sarcastic _____ in class could result in _____ .

2. My _____ to getting straight A's would be to _____ .

Be an Academic Author   **Work independently** to write two sentences. In your first sentence, use **response** with the quantifier *several*. In your second sentence, use **response** in the *singular* form.

MEANING 1 _____

_____

MEANING 2 _____

_____

> **grammar tip**
>
> Quantifiers are words that tell us how much or how many of something there is. They usually come before the noun they describe.
>
> I received **several** responses.
>
> This test has **many** questions.

Write an Academic Paragraph   **Complete** the paragraph using the correct form of **response** and original content.

When students turn in a major writing assignment like an essay or research report, teachers expect a well-organized, thoughtful _____ (1) . If a student uses proper _____ (2) and punctuation and carefully organizes his or her ideas, that student can probably expect a positive _____ (3) and a high _____ (4) from his or her teacher. However, if a student turns in a disorganized and _____ (5) draft instead of a polished paper, that student can probably expect a _____ (6) response and a poor grade. It is important to plan out your written _____ (7) before you actually start writing—otherwise, your teacher's _____ (8) will probably be to make you rewrite everything.

173

review
verb

Academic Vocabulary Toolkit

Meanings	Examples
1. to prepare for an exam by reading your notes again *Synonym:* study	**1.** Lindsay **reviewed** for the _____ by writing her notes onto _____.
2. to think about something carefully to see if changes are needed *Synonyms:* assess, evaluate	**2.** The police carefully **reviewed** the _____ before they _____ the suspect.

Forms		Family
Present:		• **Noun:** review
I/You/We/They	review	
He/She/It	reviews	
Past:	reviewed	

Word Partners

• carefully _____   The principal wants to **carefully review** the dress code changes that the students suggested at the meeting.

Verbal Practice

Talk about It   **Read** each sentence and **think** about how you would complete it.

Discuss your idea with your partner using the sentence frame.

Listen carefully to your partner's and classmates' ideas.

Write your favorite idea in the blank.

❶ You should give yourself _____ hours to **review** for a test.

❷ My favorite way to **review** for a test is to _____ .

❸ The principal should **review** our school's policy on _____ and consider changing it.

❹ The baseball coach will **review** whether or not the team needs new _____ .

Writing Practice

Collaborate — **Work with your partner** to complete the sentences using the correct form of **review** and appropriate content.

❶ You should _____ your work and fix any _____ .

❷ The principal _____ her earlier decision to suspend the students because

new evidence showed that _____ .

Your Turn — **Work independently** to complete the sentences using the correct form of **review** and appropriate content.

❶ I _____ for my last test with _____ .

❷ The panel will _____ the election results again because there was a

_____ .

Be an Academic Author — **Work independently** to write two sentences. In your first sentence, use **review** in the *simple past tense*. In your second sentence, use **review** with the modal verb *will*.

MEANING ❶ _____

_____

MEANING ❷ _____

_____

> ### grammar tip
> Modal verbs are helping verbs that give additional meaning to the main verb. *Will* can be used to express a prediction.
>
> He **will** review my work.
> They **will** win this game.

Write an Academic Paragraph — **Complete** the paragraph using the correct form of **review** and original content.

Reviewing for an important _____ **❶** may seem boring, but there are a

few ways that you can make studying more exciting. First, think of engaging ways in which you

can _____ **❷** your class materials. Try rewriting your notes or quizzing

yourself on what you can _____ **❸** from the textbook before you start

studying. Next, make flashcards by writing vocabulary words on index cards, and then invite a

_____ **❹** to _____ **❺** the words with you. Finally,

write study questions and have a family member _____ **❻** you once

you have finished studying. There are many _____ **❼** you can use when

reviewing for a test—you just have to find the one that works best for you.

revise
verb

Academic Vocabulary Toolkit

Meaning	Example
to change something *Synonym:* edit	Last week I told my parents that my _____ class was boring, but I had to **revise** my statement after we built a _____ in class!

Forms		Family
Present: I/You/We/They revise He/She/It revises *Past:* revised		• *Noun:* revision • *Adjective:* revised

Word Partners

• necessary to _____	If you want to get good grades on your papers, it is **necessary to revise** them before you turn them in.
• _____ a plan	I **revised my plans** for going to the beach this weekend after the weather forecast predicted rain.
• _____ a rule	Young children like to **revise the rules** of games so that the rules work in their favor.

Verbal Practice

Talk about It **Read** each sentence and **think** about how you would complete it.

Discuss your idea with your partner using the sentence frame.

Listen carefully to your partner's and classmates' ideas.

Write your favorite idea in the blank.

❶ I think that having _____ is helpful when I'm **revising** an essay.

❷ Will **revised** his plans to take Serena to the dance because _____ .

Writing Practice

Collaborate — **Work with your partner** to complete the sentence using the correct form of **revise** and appropriate content.

The principal is _____ the school dress code because she feels that students

_____ .

Your Turn — **Work independently** to complete the sentence using the correct form of **revise** and appropriate content.

When I _____ my essays and papers, I usually have to fix mistakes

involving _____ .

Be an Academic Author — **Work independently** to write two sentences. In your first sentence, use **revise** in the *simple present tense* with a person's name. In your second sentence, use **revise** in the *present progressive tense* and include a word partner.

❶ _____

_____

❷ _____

_____

> ## grammar tip
>
> **The present progressive tense is formed with *am/is/ are* + a verb ending in *–ing*.**
>
> Ian <u>is revising</u> his essay right now.
>
> They <u>are acting</u> in a play.

Write an Academic Paragraph — **Complete** the paragraph using the correct form of **revise** and original content.

Many students use the spell-check function on their computer to _____
❶

their writing assignments. However, using spell-check isn't enough because it can't detect all

of your possible _____ . For example, you might have spelled a word
❷

_____ but used the wrong form, such as "their" instead of "they're" or
❸

"there." In addition, spell-check can't detect problems with the logic or structure of an essay;

for example, your _____ might be poor, making it hard for your
❹

teacher to follow your argument. When you _____ something, you
❺

should read your work carefully. You can also ask a classmate to read your revision and help

you _____ it. Putting in the extra time to _____
❻   ❼

your work will likely result in a better grade.

select
verb

Academic Vocabulary Toolkit

Meaning	Example
to choose *Synonym:* pick	I usually **select** what I'm going to _____ to school the _____ before.

Forms	Family
Present: I/You/We/They select He/She/It selects *Past:* selected	• *Noun:* selection • *Adjective:* selective • *Adverb:* selectively

Word Partners

• carefully _____	The planning committee **carefully selected** the theme for this year's dance.
• randomly _____	The committee **randomly selected** 50 students to participate in the survey.
• _____ the option	When you buy this MP3 player online, you can **select the option** of having your name engraved on it.

Verbal Practice

Talk about It   **Read** each sentence and **think** about how you would complete it.

Discuss your idea with your partner using the sentence frame.

Listen carefully to your partner's and classmates' ideas.

Write your favorite idea in the blank.

❶ When I order ice cream, I usually **select** the flavor _____ .

❷ Our teacher **selected** the movie _____ for us to watch in class.

Writing Practice

Collaborate **Work with your partner** to complete the sentence using the correct form of **select** and appropriate content.

Before you _____ a new _____ , it's important to do some

research about the _____ first.

Your Turn **Work independently** to complete the sentence using the correct form of **select** and appropriate content.

I have _____ the book _____ to read next because

_____ .

Be an Academic Author **Work independently** to write two sentences. In your first sentence, use **select** in the *simple past tense*. In your second sentence, use **select** in the *present perfect tense* and include a word partner.

❶ _____

_____

❷ _____

_____

> **grammar tip**
>
> The present perfect tense is formed with *has/have* + the past participle form of the verb. To make the past participle of regular verbs, add *–ed* or *–d*.
>
> I <u>have select**ed**</u> a book.
>
> She <u>has received</u> a letter.

Write an Academic Paragraph **Complete** the paragraph using the correct form of **select** and original content.

Before you _____ a new pet, there are
                          ❶

many factors that you need to _____ . First of all, how big is your
                                          ❷

_____ ? Can you accommodate a large dog, for example? Secondly, you
          ❸

should think about how much time and attention the animal will _____ .
                                                                              ❹

Cats are independent and need less attention, but social animals like parrots require

lots of care and _____ . If you are a busy person, you might be
                          ❺

better off with a fish or a _____ . Finally, you should consider the
                                    ❻

_____ of a pet. How much will its equipment, toys, food, and veterinary
          ❼

bills cost? Once you have thought about all of these things, you are ready to go to an animal

shelter to _____ your new animal companion.
                  ❽

selection

noun

Say it: se • **lec** • tion   **Write it:** _____

Meanings	Examples
1. a choice	1. After carefully _____ all the candidates, the _____ finally made his **selection**.
2. a group of things to choose from *Synonyms:* variety, range	2. The new shoe store offers a wide **selection** of _____ .

Forms	Family
• *Singular:* selection • *Plural:* selections	• *Verb:* select • *Adjective:* selective • *Adverb:* selectively

Word Partners	
• limited ____	This music store has a **limited selection** of music—they don't have any tapes or records.
• random ____	The teacher chose a **random selection** of students to participate in the experiment.
• wide ____	The convenience store near my house has a **wide selection** of sports drinks.

Verbal Practice

Talk about It   **Read** each sentence and **think** about how you would complete it.

Discuss your idea with your partner using the sentence frame.

Listen carefully to your partner's and classmates' ideas.

Write your favorite idea in the blank.

❶ _____ is an appropriate reading **selection** for children.

❷ I've finally made my costume **selection** for the Halloween party: a _____ .

❸ I come to this store because it has a wide **selection** of _____ .

❹ The restaurant _____ has a great **selection** of _____ food.

Writing Practice

Collaborate **Work with your partner** to complete the sentences using the correct form of **selection** and appropriate content.

❶ Our grade's _____ for class president this year was _____ .

❷ Our local library has an enormous _____ of _____ .

Your Turn **Work independently** to complete the sentences using the correct form of **selection** and appropriate content.

❶ The final _____ for our new school colors were _____ .

❷ I didn't buy a _____ at the store because it had a limited _____ .

Be an Academic Author **Work independently** to write two sentences. In your first sentence, use **selection** in the *plural form*. In your second sentence, use **selection** in the *singular form* and include a word partner.

MEANING ❶ _____

_____

MEANING ❷ _____

_____

grammar tip

Count nouns name things that can be counted. Count nouns have two forms, singular and plural. To make most count nouns plural, add –s.

Who were your selection**s** for class officers?

He likes board game**s**.

Write an Academic Paragraph **Complete** the paragraph using the correct form of **selection** and original content.

Standardized _____ are difficult, but there are some strategies
                              ❶

you can follow to help you score well. Time is an important _____
                                                                ❷

to consider, so your first step should be to quickly read the directions. If you can't make a

_____ for a question, go on to the next one and come back to it
        ❸

later. If you're still not sure which answer to choose, using logic can often help you rule out

one or two choices from the _____ of answers. For example, many
                                      ❹

answer choices are designed with intentional errors such as incorrect grammar or irrelevant

_____ . You can eliminate those _____ right
        ❺   ❻

away, which will allow you to focus your time on legitimate answer possibilities. If you follow

these tips, you'll make more accurate _____ on your next test.
                                              ❼

significance
noun

Say it: sig • **nif** • i • cance   **Write it:** _____

Academic Vocabulary Toolkit

Meaning	Example
importance	When you have a crush on someone, every smile and _____ you get from him or her has special **significance**.
Antonym: insignificance	

Family

- **Verb:** signify
- **Adjective:** significant
- **Adverb:** significantly

Word Partners

• cultural _____	The Fourth of July has a lot of **cultural significance** for Americans.
• explain the _____ of something	Our teacher asked us to **explain the significance** of hip hop in modern music.
• special _____	The color black has **special significance** during funerals in the United States.

Verbal Practice

Talk about It **Read** each sentence and **think** about how you would complete it.

Discuss your idea with your partner using the sentence frame.

Listen carefully to your partner's and classmates' ideas.

Write your favorite idea in the blank.

❶ English teachers often ask students to explain the **significance** of

_____ .

❷ The sport of _____ has a lot of cultural **significance**

for Americans.

Writing Practice

Collaborate   **Work with your partner** to complete the sentence using **significance** and appropriate content.

One movie that has a lot of _____ to me is_____ because

it is about _____ .

Your Turn   **Work independently** to complete the sentence using **significance** and appropriate content.

In my house, one item of special _____ to me is my _____ .

Be an Academic Author   **Work independently** to write two sentences. In your first sentence, use **significance** with the word partner *cultural significance*. In your second sentence, use **significance** with the word partner *special significance*.

❶ _____

_____

❷ _____

_____

> ### grammar tip
> Non-count nouns name things that can't be counted. Non-count nouns have only one form. Do not add an *–s* to a non-count noun.
>
> This watch has personal **significance** to me.
>
> The **water** is frozen.

Write an Academic Paragraph   **Complete** the paragraph using **significance** and original content.

Field trips are fun, educational experiences that can significantly impact the way that

students view _____ and important world events. Field trips
      ❶

allow students to explore _____ that have had great cultural
      ❷

and personal _____ for people throughout history. For example,
      ❸

in a museum you might see items that people used to celebrate births, weddings, and

_____ . Some museums also feature the mummies of important
      ❹

_____ in history, such as King Tut! Field trips can help students
      ❺

understand the _____ of the past and its impact on the
      ❻

_____ . Additionally, learning about history and other cultures also
      ❼

helps students appreciate the _____ of events and traditions in their
      ❽

own lives and cultures.

significant
adjective

▶ **Say it:** sig • **nif** • i • cant   **Write it:** _____

Academic Vocabulary Toolkit

Meanings	Examples
1. important	1. When _____ became president, it was a **significant** event because he was the first _____ elected president.
2. a large amount of something **Synonym:** big **Antonym:** insignificant	2. It's not a good idea to drink _____ before bed because it has a **significant** amount of _____ .

Family

- **Noun:** significance
- **Verb:** signify
- **Adverb:** significantly

Word Partners

• _____ amount of	I need a **significant amount of** sleep every night in order to function.
• _____ difference between	There is a **significant difference between** golf and ice hockey.
• _____ role	Pollutants and carcinogens play a **significant role** in the development of cancer.

Verbal Practice

Talk about It   **Read** each sentence and **think** about how you would complete it.

Discuss your idea with your partner using the sentence frame.

Listen carefully to your partner's and classmates' ideas.

Write your favorite idea in the blank.

❶ One **significant** invention from the past 100 years is _____ .

❷ My _____ has played a **significant** role in my life.

❸ A **significant** number of students at this school wear _____ every day.

❹ I have a **significant** amount of homework for my _____ class.

Writing Practice

Collaborate **Work with your partner** to complete the sentences using **significant** and appropriate content.

1 Creative activities like _____ are a _____ part of my life

because they _____ .

2 The class that I've had the most _____ improvement in this year

is _____ . My grade went up to _____ .

Your Turn **Work independently** to complete the sentences using **significant** and appropriate content.

1 One of the most _____ events in my life was when I

_____ .

2 I eat a _____ amount of _____ every week.

Be an Academic Author **Work independently** to write two sentences. In your first sentence, use **significant** with the word partner *significant role*. In your second sentence, use **significant** with the word partner *significant amount of*.

MEANING 1 _____

_____

MEANING 2 _____

_____

grammar tip

Amount of is a quantifier used with non-count nouns. It describes how much of a noun there is. With count nouns, use the quantifier *number of*.

This soup has a **significant amount of salt** in it.

There are a **significant number of students** here.

Write an Academic Paragraph **Complete** the paragraph using **significant** and original content.

Many people in the United States struggle with obesity.

Obesity is a _____ 1 concern because it can cause serious health

_____ 2 such as diabetes and knee pain. Losing weight is not

_____ 3 to do, but there are some small changes that anyone

can try in order to make a _____ 4 difference in their health. For

example, drinking water instead of soda can drastically _____ 5

your daily calorie intake. In addition, taking the stairs instead of the elevator burns more

_____ 6 and builds fat-burning muscle. These are small steps, but they

can have a _____ 7 effect on people's health.

185

similar
adjective

▶ **Say it:** **sim** • i • lar   **Write it:** _____

Academic Vocabulary Toolkit

Meaning	Example
almost the same	The Smith _____ look **similar**, but they _____ very differently from each other.
Synonyms: like, alike	
Antonym: dissimilar	

Family

Noun: similarity
Adverb: similarly

Word Partners

- _____ pattern   All mammals follow a **similar pattern** of development—they drink milk as babies and grow fur or hair on their bodies.

- _____ problem   Last year insects ate many of the fruits and vegetables in our garden, and we're having a **similar problem** this year.

- _____ results   When our class tried the experiment a second time, we got **similar results**.

Verbal Practice

Talk about It   **Read** each sentence and **think** about how you would complete it.

Discuss your idea with your partner using the sentence frame.

Listen carefully to your partner's and classmates' ideas.

Write your favorite idea in the blank.

❶ My friends and I have **similar** interests; we all like _____

and _____ .

❷ Taking care of a puppy is **similar** to taking care of a baby because they both need

_____ .

Writing Practice

Collaborate **Work with your partner** to complete the sentence using **similar** and appropriate content.

Our school's _____ team followed a _____ pattern as last

year—they won about _____ percent of the games that they played.

Your Turn **Work independently** to complete the sentence using **similar** and appropriate content.

People often say my _____ and I have _____ characteristics

because we both _____ .

Be an Academic Author **Work independently** to write two sentences using **similar**. In your first sentence, use **similar** with a *plural noun*. In your second sentence, use **similar** with a *singular noun*.

❶ _____

_____

❷ _____

_____

> **grammar tip**
>
> **Adjectives do not have plural forms. Do not add an –s to adjectives when they describe plural nouns.**
>
> <u>similar</u> result**s**
>
> <u>loud</u> dog**s**

Write an Academic Paragraph **Complete** the paragraph using **similar** and original content.

Reality TV is a fast-growing phenomenon. Many people are fascinated by the

_____ of reality stars because the events that they see on TV
      ❶

are either very _____ or completely dissimilar to their own
      ❷

experiences. For example, reality shows that focus on fitness or weight loss are very

_____ because many people have similarly struggled with
      ❸

_____ . However, sometimes reality shows are popular because
      ❹

the stars have lives that are _____ or extraordinary in some way.
      ❺

For instance, reality shows about celebrities offer a glimpse into the lives of people who

are incredibly _____ or famous. Reality TV will continue to grow in
      ❻

popularity as long as there are people who are interested in _____
      ❼

the lives of others.

similarity

noun

Academic Vocabulary Toolkit

Meaning	Example
a likeness or sameness *Synonym:* resemblance	It's funny when dogs and their _____ share physical **similarities**.

Forms	Family
• *Singular:* similarity • *Plural:* similarities	• *Adjective:* similar • *Adverb:* similarly

Word Partners	
• share _____ s	Siblings **share similarities** in appearance but usually have different personalities.
• _____ s between	There are many **similarities between** baseball and softball.
• striking _____	There is a **striking similarity** between squids and octopuses.

Verbal Practice

Talk about It   **Read** each sentence and **think** about how you would complete it.

Discuss your idea with your partner using the sentence frame.

Listen carefully to your partner's and classmates' ideas.

Write your favorite idea in the blank.

❶ There are many **similarities** between the video games

_____ and _____ .

❷ If you met my family, you would see a **similarity** between me and

my _____ .

Writing Practice

Collaborate   **Work with your partner** to complete the sentence using the correct form of **similarity** and appropriate content.

There is a striking _____ between the music of _____

and the music of _____ .

Your Turn   **Work independently** to complete the sentence using the correct form of **similarity** and appropriate content.

My classmates and I share many _____ ; for example, we all

_____ .

Be an Academic Author   **Work independently** to write two sentences. In your first sentence, use **similarity** in the *plural form* with the quantifier *many*. In your second sentence, use **similarity** in the *singular form*.

❶ _____

_____

❷ _____

_____

> ### grammar tip
> Quantifiers are words that tell us how much or how many of something there is. They usually come before the noun they describe.
>
> There are <u>many</u> similarities between siblings.
>
> We have a <u>few</u> ideas.

Write an Academic Paragraph   **Complete** the paragraph using the correct form of **similarity** and original content.

There are many _____ ❶ between having a part-time job and

going to classes at school. One _____ ❷ is that you are responsible for

completing assigned _____ ❸ . Another _____ ❹

you might discover is that you need to listen carefully to instructions from your boss and your

teacher. Jobs and school are also similar because you must arrive on time, and you shouldn't

_____ ❺ while you are in class or working. Finally, the most important

_____ ❻ between having a job and going to school is that both require

a significant amount of time and effort. Ultimately, you will find that working part-time and

going to school, while difficult, can be very _____ ❼ .

subjective
adjective

▶ **Say it:** sub • **jec** • tive

Write it: _____

<table>
<tr><th colspan="2">Meaning</th><th colspan="2">Example</th></tr>
<tr><td colspan="2">based on personal feelings instead of facts

Synonym: biased
Antonym: objective</td><td colspan="2">Carla's opinion of Mr. Bell is

subjective because he is

her _____ .</td></tr>
</table>

Academic Vocabulary Toolkit

Family
Adverb: subjectively

Word Partners	
• highly _____	Taste in art is **highly subjective** because everyone has different feelings about what they see.

Verbal Practice

Talk about It **Read** each sentence and **think** about how you would complete it.

Discuss your idea with your partner using the sentence frame.

Listen carefully to your partner's and classmates' ideas.

Write your favorite idea in the blank.

❶ I could tell you a lot of great things about the city of _____

because I've spent so much time there, but my opinion would be **subjective**.

❷ Judges should not be **subjective** when they are _____ .

Writing Practice

Collaborate **Work with your partner** to complete the sentence using **subjective** and appropriate content.

The best brand of _____ is a _____ opinion.

Your Turn **Work independently** to complete the sentence using **subjective** and appropriate content.

Sometimes I wonder if teachers are _____ about the grades they give because

it seems like some students always do _____ no matter what.

Be an Academic Author **Work independently** to write two sentences. In your first sentence, use **subjective** with a *singular noun*. In your second sentence, use **subjective** with the word partner *highly subjective*.

❶ _____

_____

❷ _____

_____

> ### grammar tip
> **Adjectives do not have plural forms. Do not add an −*s* to adjectives when they describe plural nouns.**
>
> <u>subjective</u> opinion**s**
>
> <u>loud</u> dog**s**

Write an Academic Paragraph **Complete** the paragraph using **subjective** and original content.

All opinions are _____ **❶** by nature. However, when you

_____ **❷** a persuasive paper or an essay for school, you have to keep

your personal _____ **❸** under control while trying to persuade your

reader. Persuasive writing certainly includes opinions, but your _____ **❹**

must express your point of view without sounding overly subjective. Try starting your paper

with the words "I think…" or "I believe…" Then, cross out those two words, and you will no

longer have a thesis statement that sounds _____ **❺** . As you continue to

write, you should _____ **❻** your thesis with facts and observations that

strengthen your argument. Eliminating _____ **❼** language from your

writing will make it more convincing.

tradition
noun

▶ **Say it:** tra • **di** • tion   **Write it:** _____

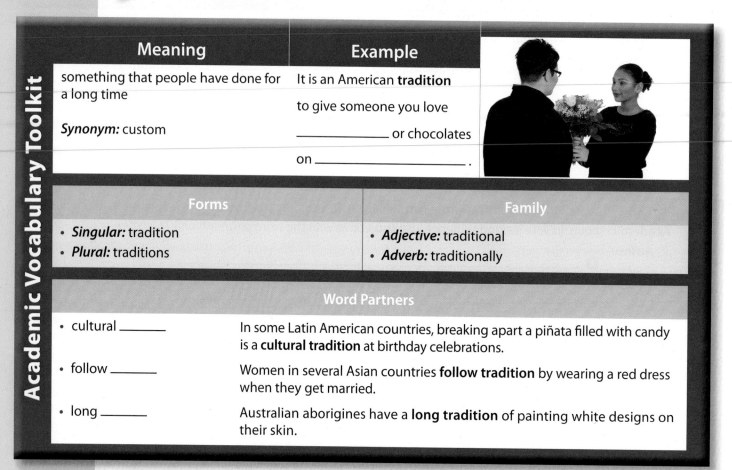

Meaning	Example
something that people have done for a long time **Synonym:** custom	It is an American **tradition** to give someone you love _____ or chocolates on _____ .

Forms	Family
• **Singular:** tradition • **Plural:** traditions	• **Adjective:** traditional • **Adverb:** traditionally

Word Partners

• cultural _____	In some Latin American countries, breaking apart a piñata filled with candy is a **cultural tradition** at birthday celebrations.
• follow _____	Women in several Asian countries **follow tradition** by wearing a red dress when they get married.
• long _____	Australian aborigines have a **long tradition** of painting white designs on their skin.

Academic Vocabulary Toolkit

Verbal Practice

Talk about It **Read** each sentence and **think** about how you would complete it.

Discuss your idea with your partner using the sentence frame.

Listen carefully to your partner's and classmates' ideas.

Write your favorite idea in the blank.

❶ My favorite holiday **tradition** is _____ .

❷ Our school has an annual **tradition** of _____ .

Writing Practice

Collaborate **Work with your partner** to complete the sentence using the correct form of **tradition** and appropriate content.

It is a cultural _____ in the country of _____ for people to

celebrate the holiday of _____ by _____ .

Your Turn **Work independently** to complete the sentence using the correct form of **tradition** and appropriate content.

One _____ that my family follows is _____ .

Be an Academic Author **Work independently** to write two sentences. In your first sentence, use **tradition** in the *singular form*. In your second sentence, use **tradition** in the *plural form* and include a word partner.

❶ _____

_____

❷ _____

_____

> ## grammar tip
> Count nouns name things that can be counted. Count nouns have two forms, singular and plural. To make most count nouns plural, add –s.
>
> My family follows many holiday traditions.
>
> He likes board games.

Write an Academic Paragraph **Complete** the paragraph using the correct form of **tradition** and original content.

Every November, the residents of Lop Buri, Thailand, prepare for a unique cultural

_____ ❶ : the Monkey Buffet Festival. On the last Sunday in November,

Lop Buri's top chefs _____ ❷ thousands of pounds of colorful fruits,

vegetables, and treats. The feast is laid out in _____ ❸ displays on buffet

tables in the sacred Phra Prang Sam Yot Buddhist temple. Local residents and tourists then

watch as hundreds of macaque monkeys, which live and roam freely in Lop Buri, come and

_____ ❹ the treats. This unusual _____ ❺ is a

way to honor the monkeys, who are believed to bring good _____ ❻

to Lop Buri. This _____ ❼ attracts thousands of tourists to the city every

year and is one of the most entertaining (and messy) festivals in the world.

unique
adjective

Write it: _____

Academic Vocabulary Toolkit

Meaning	Example
not like anything else **Synonyms:** special, one-of-a-kind	No two _____ are exactly alike; each one is **unique**.

Family

- **Noun:** uniqueness
- **Adverb:** uniquely

Word Partners

• _____ experience	Traveling to the Dominican Republic and participating in a study abroad program will be a **unique experience** for our Spanish club.
• _____ feature	One **unique feature** of elephants is their long trunk.
• _____ opportunity	Performing in the Thanksgiving Day parade is a **unique opportunity** for our chorus.

Verbal Practice

Talk about It **Read** each sentence and **think** about how you would complete it.

Discuss your idea with your partner using the sentence frame.

Listen carefully to your partner's and classmates' ideas.

Write your favorite idea in the blank.

❶ The singer _____ has a **unique** voice that is easy to recognize.

❷ One **unique** piece of clothing that I own is a _____ .

Writing Practice

Collaborate   **Work with your partner** to complete the sentence using **unique** and appropriate content.

The _____ is a _____ animal because it

_____ .

Your Turn   **Work independently** to complete the sentence using **unique** and appropriate content.

Of all the students at my school, I have a _____ perspective on the topic

of _____ because I _____ .

Be an Academic Author   **Work independently** to write two sentences. In your first sentence, use **unique** with a *singular noun*. In your second sentence, use **unique** with a *plural noun*.

❶ _____

_____

❷ _____

_____

> ### grammar tip
>
> **Adjectives do not have plural forms. Do not add an −s to adjectives when they describe plural nouns.**
>
> <u>unique</u> style**s**
>
> <u>loud</u> dog**s**

Write an Academic Paragraph   **Complete** the paragraph using **unique** and original content.

Every person has _____❶_____ fingerprints, including identical twins.

Fingerprints are _____❷_____ by epidermal ridges, or raised portions of skin

on the tips of the fingers. These ridges are completely _____❸_____ and

specific to one person. _____❹_____ marks similar to fingerprints can also

be found on other parts of the body, including toes and the soles of the feet. The uniqueness

of fingerprints is often used for identification _____❺_____ , such as in crime

scene investigations and missing person cases. Investigators _____❻_____

fingerprints using special chemicals that make fingerprints easy to see. Police

can then compare the fingerprints to a database or to fingerprints that they have

_____❼_____ from another person.

valid
adjective

▶ *Say it:* **val** · id   *Write it:* _____

Meanings	Examples	
1. good or usable *Antonym:* invalid	**1.** With a **valid** _____ card, you can check out books and DVDs.	**Student Library Card** Student Name JANE MONTGOMERY Student I.D. Number 0578910612AF VALID 2015-2016
2. reasonable or sensible *Antonym:* invalid	**2.** Joey gave a **valid** _____ for being late to class.	MY BUS HAD A FLAT TIRE!

Family

Nouns: validity, validation
Verb: validate

Word Partners

• _____ argument	One **valid argument** for watching the news is that you should be informed about world events.
• _____ point	I don't agree with you entirely on this issue, but you've made a **valid point.**
• _____ reason	Terry gave a **valid reason** for not turning in her homework: her dog actually ate it and had to go to the vet!

Verbal Practice

Talk about It   **Read** each sentence and **think** about how you would complete it.

Discuss your idea with your partner using the sentence frame.

Listen carefully to your partner's and classmates' ideas.

Write your favorite idea in the blank.

❶ You can get into trouble for driving without a **valid** _____ .

❷ Items like _____ usually have an expiration date to show how long they are **valid.**

❸ One **valid** reason for failing a student is if he or she doesn't _____ .

❹ _____ isn't a **valid** excuse for being late.

Writing Practice

Collaborate **Work with your partner** to complete the sentence using **valid** and appropriate content.

One _____ argument for owning a cell phone is that

_____ .

Your Turn **Work independently** to complete the sentence using **valid** and appropriate content.

A _____ reason for missing school is if you _____ .

Be an Academic Author **Work independently** to write two sentences. In your first sentence, use **valid** with a *singular noun*. In your second sentence, use **valid** with a *plural noun*.

❶ _____

_____

❷ _____

_____

> **grammar tip**
>
> **Adjectives do not have plural forms. Do not add an –s to adjectives when they describe plural nouns.**
>
> valid reasons
>
> loud dogs

Write an Academic Paragraph **Complete** the paragraph using **valid** and original content.

We all have various reasons for not meeting people's expectations. But are your reasons _____ ❶ ? When you have a _____ ❷ explanation for not meeting an expectation, people are usually more willing to _____ ❸ you. For example, most teachers would consider a death in your family as a _____ ❹ reason for not turning in _____ ❺ because that is a situation beyond your control. But failing to turn in something because you _____ ❻ all night is definitely an invalid excuse; it represents a bad choice you made. Before you decide not to do something, _____ ❼ the repercussions and whether you want to disappoint someone by giving them a poor excuse.

variety
noun

▶ **Say it:** va • **ri** • e • ty   **Write it:** _____

Academic Vocabulary Toolkit

Meaning	Example
different types	A _____ features a **variety** of different stores and _____ .

Forms	Family
• **Singular:** variety • **Plural:** varieties	• **Verb:** vary • **Adjective:** various • **Adverb:** variously

Word Partners	
• offer a _____ of	Our school **offers a variety of** meals for lunch every week.
• _____ of reasons	There are a **variety of reasons** why you should brush your teeth every day.
• wide _____ of	This ice cream shop has a **wide variety of** flavors.

Verbal Practice

Talk about It   **Read** each sentence and **think** about how you would complete it.

Discuss your idea with your partner using the sentence frame.

Listen carefully to your partner's and classmates' ideas.

Write your favorite idea in the blank.

❶ I have relatives living in a **variety** of places: _____

and _____ are two of them.

❷ In history class, we have studied a **variety** of important events, such as

_____ .

198

Writing Practice

Collaborate **Work with your partner** to complete the sentence using the correct form of **variety** and appropriate content.

Our school offers a _____ of extracurricular activities, such as

_____ and _____ .

Your Turn **Work independently** to complete the sentence using the correct form of **variety** and appropriate content.

There are many _____ of fruits in the United States, such as

_____ and _____ , but my favorite is _____ .

Be an Academic Author **Work independently** to write two sentences. In your first sentence, use **variety** in the *singular form* and include a word partner. In your second sentence, use **variety** in the *plural form*.

❶ _____

_____

❷ _____

_____

> ### grammar tip
> To form the plural of a noun that ends in a consonant + *y*, change the *y* to *i* and add *–es*.
> variety—variet**ies**
> puppy—pupp**ies**

Write an Academic Paragraph **Complete** the paragraph using the correct form of **variety** and original content.

Grocery stores in the United States now offer a wider _____ of
❶

foods than ever before due to greater _____ to foods grown in other
❷

countries. Exotic fruits such as mangoes and _____ that were once
❸

only accessible to Americans on vacation are now plentiful in the produce section. Other

examples include foods from Asia such as tofu and miso, which are now commonly offered in

_____ restaurants and also in grocery store aisles. Many Americans
❹

have _____ incorporated these foods into their diets; besides the
❺

delicious taste, these foods offer a _____ of nutritional benefits.
❻

For example, mangoes are rich in vitamin C, while tofu _____
❼

bone-strengthening calcium.

vary
verb

▶ **Say it:** var • y   **Write it:** _____

Academic Vocabulary Toolkit

Meanings	Examples
1. to differ	1. _____ **varies** from person to person.
2. to change	2. School _____ **vary** their menus every day.

Cafeteria Menu
Monday..Hamburgers
Tuesday..........Tacos
Wednesday......Pizza
Thursday.....Lasagna
Friday.....Sloppy Joes

Forms	Family
Present: I/You/We/They vary He/She/It varies **Past:** varied	• **Noun:** variation • **Adjectives:** varied, varying, various, variable

Word Partners

• _____ considerably   In the United States, the cost of gasoline **varies considerably** depending on where you live.

• _____ widely   Our football team's performance **varies widely** every year.

Verbal Practice

Talk about It   **Read** each sentence and **think** about how you would complete it.

Discuss your idea with your partner using the sentence frame.

Listen carefully to your partner's and classmates' ideas.

Write your favorite idea in the blank.

❶ The weather here **varies** considerably from mild to _____ .

❷ The classes I am taking this semester **vary** from _____

to _____ .

❸ If you're bored after school, you should **vary** your routine and

_____ .

❹ My desire to _____ **varies** from day to day.

Writing Practice

Collaborate Work with your partner to complete the sentences using the correct form of **vary** and appropriate content.

❶ The price of a bottle of water _____ considerably when you buy it from a vending machine versus when you buy it from a _____ .

❷ Our school _____ the _____ that are available each semester.

Your Turn Work independently to complete the sentences using the correct form of **vary** and appropriate content.

❶ My taste in _____ doesn't _____ much from my friends'.

❷ The last time I _____ my hairstyle was _____ .

Be an Academic Author Work independently to write two sentences. In your first sentence, use **vary** in the *simple present tense* and include a word partner. In your second sentence, use **vary** in the *simple past tense*.

MEANING ❶ _____

_____

MEANING ❷ _____

_____

grammar tip

To make the simple past tense of verbs ending in a consonant + *y*, change the *y* to *i* and add –*ed*.

Her grades vari**ed** from mine.

I **tried** the coffee but didn't like it.

Write an Academic Paragraph Complete the paragraph using the correct form of **vary** and original content.

High school experiences _____ ❶

from country to country. In the United States, students attend high school for four

_____ ❷ . However, in _____ ❸ such as Iran and

Mexico, high school lasts for only three years, while high school in Scotland takes six years! High

schools also _____ ❹ in the types of classes they offer. For example, in

Finland, students have the _____ ❺ to attend vocational school and learn

a trade or to go to a regular high school with academic classes. Finally, the dress code for high

school students around the world _____ ❻ . Students in Malaysia and New

Zealand typically _____ ❼ uniforms, but students in the U.S. often do not.

Photo Credits

Grammar Lessons

Singular Nouns and the Simple Present Tense

Sample Sentences

1. Broccoli contains a lot of vitamins.

2. She listens to her messages before lunch.

3. Elena babysits her little brother on Tuesdays while her mother goes to yoga class.

4. My cousin believes in UFOs.

Simple Present Tense

The simple present tense has two forms: the base form and the –s form.

Subject	Verb
I You We They	read.
He/She/It	reads.

Singular Nouns and the Simple Present Tense

- Singular means "one." A singular noun is one of something: a book, Wendy Brown, the school, Miami.

- In the simple present, use the –s form of the verb when the subject is a singular noun or *he, she,* or *it.* This is called the "third-person singular."

Spelling Changes in the Simple Present Tense

- When the base form of the verb ends in *s, sh, ch,* or *x,* add –es.

- When the base form of the verb ends in a consonant + *y,* change the *y* to *i* and add –es.

- Add –es to *go* and *do.*

- *Have* is irregular. The –s form of *have* is *has.*

Base Form	–s Form
kiss	kisses
catch	catches
fix	fixes
cry	cries
go	goes
have	has

Collaborate **Work with your partner** to complete the sentences using the simple present tense form of each verb and original content.

❶ make   In our class, _____ is the student who

_____ everyone laugh.

❷ go/listen   During lunch, _____ , the principal of our

school, _____ to the nurse's office and

_____ to hip-hop music.

❸ try/act   A good student always _____

his or her best and _____ respectfully.

❹ mix   Leo often _____ together condiments

like _____ and _____ and eats

them with french fries.

❺ have   At least one student in this class _____ a

problem understanding _____ .

Your Turn   **Work independently** to complete the sentences using the simple present tense form of each verb.

❶ watch   Every night, Kayla _____ about three hours

of TV.

❷ want   He _____ his parents to buy a new car.

❸ pass/say   When she _____ me in the hall, she never

_____ anything.

❹ go/do   My sister _____ into the bathroom every

morning and _____ her hair for about

an hour!

❺ think/crush He _____ he's so strong when he

_____ a soda can.

Plural Forms of Nouns

Sample Sentences

❶ Most teachers arrive at school before 7:00 a.m.

❷ Some classes have over 30 students.

❸ Zhi went to the store to buy potatoes and tomatoes.

❹ All the babies in the hospital were boys.

Forms of Plural Nouns

- To form the plural of most count nouns, add –s to the singular form.

- To form the plural of nouns that end in ss, ch, sh, or x, add –es.

- To form the plural of nouns that end in a consonant + y, change the y to i and add –es.

- To form the plural of most nouns that end in a consonant + o, add –es.

- Some singular nouns that end in –is form the plural by changing the –is to –es.

- Some nouns have irregular plural forms.

Singular	Plural
animal	animals
kiss	kisses
peach	peaches
box	boxes
party	parties
echo	echoes
crisis	crises
child	children

Collaborate Work with your partner to complete the sentences using the correct form of each noun.

❶ penguin   On our field trip to the zoo, we saw dozens of _____ .

❷ potato/   My favorite foods include mashed

  strawberry   _____ and _____ .

❸ eye   Selena drew a picture of a monster with four _____ .

❹ skirt   In our class, three people are wearing _____ .

❺ inch   Cesar is five feet nine _____ tall.

Your Turn Work independently to complete the sentences using the correct form of each noun.

❶ house   On my street, three _____ are painted white.

❷ church   There are several _____ in my neighborhood.

❸ hero   Many brave _____ died in World War II.

❹ lady   In the past, some _____ wore long skirts.

❺ child   Dozens of _____ are playing in the park.

Quantifiers

Sample Sentences

❶ None of the books on the reading list is in the library.

❷ A superhero fights for both truth and justice.

❸ Many people in this class speak Mandarin.

❹ Take a lot of food and water when you go camping.

Placement of Quantifiers

- Quantifiers are words or expressions that tell how much or how many of a noun there is.

- Quantifiers go before the noun and before adjectives describing the noun.

- We use quantifiers with count and non-count nouns. Some quantifiers can only be used with count nouns.

Quantifier	Count	Non-count
no	X	X
none of	X	
both	X	X
a few	X	
several	X	
a lot of	X	X
a number of	X	
many	X	
numerous	X	

Collaborate **Work with a partner** to complete the sentences using appropriate quantifiers and original content.

❶ In our class, _____ students want to become _____ .

❷ Mario went _____ and broke _____ his legs.

❸ _____ the movies at my local theater sound _____ .

❹ Jordan found _____ pencils at the bottom of her

_____ .

❺ Last night my _____ baked _____ cookies.

Your Turn **Work independently** to complete the sentences using appropriate quantifiers and original content.

❶ There are _____ televisions in my _____ .

❷ My dream house has _____ _____ .

❸ On the test, _____ the possible answers to the first question seemed

_____ .

❹ You need to take _____ classes in science and

_____ if you want to graduate.

❺ I like to drink _____ with _____ sugar.

Simple Past Tense of Regular Verbs

Sample Sentences

❶ Yesterday at the football game, Franco kicked the winning field goal.

❷ I moved to the United States from Haiti ten years ago.

❸ My dad fried catfish for dinner last night.

❹ We shopped at that store every week until it closed.

Simple Past Tense of Regular Verbs

- The form of the simple past tense is the same for all persons.

- To form the simple past tense of most regular verbs, add –ed to the base form of the verb.

Base Form	Simple Past Tense
listen	listened
start	started
open	opened
want	wanted

- Add –d to regular verbs that end in e.

- For verbs that end in a consonant + y, change the y to i and add –ed.

- Some verbs that end in a consonant form the past tense by doubling the final consonant and then adding –ed.

Base Form	Simple Past Tense
smile	smiled
cry	cried
permit	permitted

Collaborate **Work with your partner** to complete the sentences using the simple past tense form of each verb and original content.

① sub Last week, when our _____ teacher was sick,

_____ _____ for her.

② ask/cook My mother _____ me to make dinner, so I

_____ my favorite meal: _____ .

③ carry Because it was so heavy, I _____ my grandmother's

_____ upstairs for her.

④ die/pass/crash We almost _____ last night when a car

_____ us on the right and _____

into us.

⑤ attend All the students _____ the _____ .

Your Turn **Work independently** to complete the sentences using the simple past tense form of each verb.

① wait Yesterday I _____ at the bus stop for over

an hour.

② occur Over 25 years ago, a nuclear disaster _____

in Europe.

③ worry Before she took the test, Jill _____ that she

might fail.

④ live Shakespeare _____ in England from 1564

to 1616.

⑤ admit/rob The criminal finally _____ that he

_____ the bank last week.

209

Present Progressive Tense

Sample Sentences

❶ We are studying vocabulary.

❷ I am listening to music at the moment.

❸ Mr. Ortiz is losing weight because he is exercising every day.

❹ Look, it is raining.

Forms of the Present Progressive Tense

The present progressive tense is formed with *am/is/are* and a verb ending in *–ing*.

Subject	*be*	Verb + *–ing*
I	am	reading.
You/We/They	are	studying.
He/She/It	is	laughing.

Uses of the Present Progressive Tense

• Use the present progressive tense for an action that is happening right now.

• Use the present progressive tense to show a long-term action that is in progress.

• We do not usually use the present progressive tense with nonaction verbs like *seem, see, like, know,* and *want*. For example, we do not say: *I am liking the weather.*

Spelling Changes

• If the verb ends in a consonant + *e*, drop the *e* before adding *–ing*.

• For a one-syllable verb that ends in a consonant + vowel + consonant (CVC), double the final consonant and add *–ing*.

• Do not double a final *w, x,* or *y*.

• For a two-syllable verb that ends in a CVC, double the final consonant only if the last syllable is stressed.

Verb	*–ing* Form
dance	dancing
stop	stopping
stay	staying
permit	permitting
offer	offering

Collaborate **Work with your partner** to complete the sentences using the present progressive form of each verb and original content.

❶ wear   Tanya's clothes are crazy; today she _____ purple

shoes and _____ .

❷ shop   I _____ for a new _____ for next

week's _____ .

❸ bake   My mother _____ a cake for

_____ .

❹ begin   To prepare for their trip to _____ , Alanna and Rob

_____ to study Spanish.

❺ make   Many students _____ plans for

_____ .

Your Turn **Work independently** to complete the sentences using the present progressive form of each verb and original content.

❶ sit   Today in class I _____ behind

_____ .

❷ plan   My friends _____ a surprise party for

_____ .

❸ stay   Hailey _____ after school today because she

_____ .

❹ listen   In music class, the students _____ to the music of

_____ .

❺ offer   This week the cafeteria _____ everyone a free

_____ .

Present Perfect Tense

Sample Sentences

1. I have played football since I was seven.
2. She has promised to help me with my essay.
3. Sophia has already spoken to her parents about getting her driver's license.
4. We have just finished eating lunch.

Forms of the Present Perfect Tense

Subject	have/has	Past Participle
I You We They	have	played.
He/She/It	has	promised.

- The present perfect tense is formed with *has/have* + the past participle form of the verb.
- To make the past participle of regular verbs, add *–ed* or *–d*.
- Use *have* with *I, you, we, they,* and plural nouns.
- Use *has* with *he, she, it,* and singular nouns.

When to Use the Simple Past or Present Perfect

- Use the **simple past tense** when the action started and finished in the past.
- Use the **present perfect tense** when the action began in the past but continues into the present.
- We often use the **present perfect** with time words such as *already, since, always,* and *never*.
- We can also use the **present perfect** to talk about the recent past. Words like *just* and *recently* show the recent past.
- We also use the **present perfect** to talk about repeated actions in the past if the action might occur again in the future.

Collaborate **Work with your partner** to complete the sentences using the present perfect form of each verb and original content.

❶ read   Every day this week we _____ _____ poems in class.

❷ hear   Can you believe that she _____ never _____ of _____ ?

❸ live   How long _____ you _____ in your home?

❹ finish   I _____ just _____ reading _____ ; it's an amazing book.

❺ be   Where is _____ ? He _____ _____ absent a lot recently.

Your Turn **Work independently** to complete the sentences using the present perfect form of each verb.

❶ work   My mother _____ _____ for the same company since 2005.

❷ go   I _____ already _____ to the principal's office many times.

❸ live   Martin _____ _____ in California for four years.

❹ fall   Tara keeps ice skating even though she _____ _____ many times.

❺ return   Alberto _____ just _____ from visiting his cousins in Puerto Rico.

Adverbs of Frequency

❶ Marco never goes to the pool; he can't swim.

❷ I always study the night before a test.

❸ Tiana is frequently late for volleyball practice.

❹ Usually I buy lunch at school.

Meanings of Adverbs of Frequency

Adverbs of frequency show how often something happens.

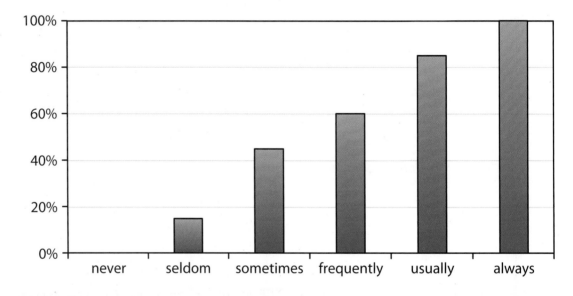

Placement of Adverbs of Frequency

- Adverbs of frequency come after the verb *be* but before other verbs.

- Adverbs of frequency go after a modal verb.

- Some adverbs of frequency, such as *usually, often, frequently, sometimes,* and *generally,* can also go at the beginning of a sentence.

Collaborate   **Work with your partner** to complete the sentences using appropriate adverbs of frequency and original content.

➊ I _____ brush my teeth before I _____ .

➋ Students in this class are _____ late because _____ .

➌ _____ , I have to agree with people who say _____ .

➍ When I see my _____ on the street, I _____ stop and talk to them.

➎ My family _____ goes to restaurants—maybe

_____ times a _____ .

Your Turn   **Work independently** to complete the sentences using appropriate adverbs of frequency and original content.

➊ Now that I have _____ , I _____ watch TV.

➋ My brother loves his _____ . You _____ see him without it.

➌ She _____ gets a haircut; her hair is _____ .

➍ People in my family _____ speak _____ .

➎ _____ , I prefer to communicate with my friends by

_____ .

Modal Verbs

Sample Sentences

1. If he has time, Kevin may help me move.

2. Mia can speak Russian, but she can't speak German.

3. If it rains, I might not go to the beach.

4. You should stay home and study tonight.

Modals: Form and Placement

- Modals do not have *–s, –ed,* or *–ing* endings.

- The base form of the verb follows the modal verb.

- Make modals negative by placing *not* right after the modal.

Modals and Their Meanings

Modal verbs give additional meaning to the main verb.

	Use	Example
can	ability request	Alex can walk on his hands. Can I talk to you later?
could	future possibility request past ability	This could end in a disaster. Could you speak more slowly? Once I could play the violin, but I've forgotten how.
may	permission future possibility	You may wait outside my office. Emilia may win a medal if she continues to practice.
might	possibility	If I ask nicely, my parents might let me have the car tonight.
must	obligation	Daniel must visit his grandmother on Sunday.
should	advice	You should eat more vegetables.
will	prediction promise	Coach thinks we will win the state championship this year. I will call you tomorrow.
would	preference invitation	I would like iced tea, please. Would you play tennis with me?

Work with your partner to complete the sentences using appropriate modals and base forms of verbs and original content.

❶ During a test, you _____ not _____ .

❷ I promise I _____ _____ everything I can

to _____ .

❸ If you want to make the basketball team, you _____

_____ .

❹ My best friend _____ _____ very well, but I'm

hopeless!

❺ In the future, people _____ be able to _____ .

Your Turn **Work independently** to complete the sentences using appropriate modals and base forms of verbs and original content.

❶ I want to go to the _____ , but Jayden _____

_____ to go to the mall.

❷ Your _____ is so old; you _____

_____ a new one.

❸ I'm so busy—_____ you _____ this for me?

❹ Raul _____ _____ to Europe this summer, but he

doesn't want to.

❺ Zoe and I are going _____ ; _____ you like to come

with us?

Adjectives

Sample Sentences

❶ Every night my father cooks a healthy dinner.

❷ Look at the people walking down the busy streets.

❸ You should take a nap—you look sleepy.

❹ Last summer I read many fascinating novels.

Adjectives: Placement and Number

- An adjective describes a noun.

- An adjective usually comes before the noun it describes.

- Adjectives can come after the verb be and verbs like *look, sound, smell, taste,* and *feel*.

- Adjectives are always singular, even if they describe a plural noun. Do not add –s to adjectives that describe plural nouns.

Collaborate   **Work with a partner** to complete the sentences using appropriate adjectives and original content.

❶ We watched a _____ sunset.

❷ After spending lots of money at the _____ , Sam has a

_____ smile.

❸ The _____ smells _____ ; bring it outside.

❹ Russ and Amy are _____ musicians who play _____ .

❺ Canada and _____ are _____ countries.

Your Turn   **Work independently** to complete the following sentences using appropriate adjectives and original content.

❶ I usually listen to music like _____ that is _____

and _____ .

❷ Jack and Devon are _____ guys who like baseball and

_____ .

❸ This playground has _____ rides and is painted

_____ colors.

❹ Deserts are _____ places.

❺ _____ is a/an _____ last name

in _____ .